The Teller's Tale

The Teller's Tale

Lives of the Classic Fairy Tale Writers

Edited by

Sophie Raynard

Published by State University of New York Press, Albany

For information, contact State University of New York Press, Albany, NY
www.sunypress.edu

Production by Eileen Nizer
Marketing by Anne M. Valentine

Library of Congress Cataloging-in-Publication Data

The teller's tale : lives of the classic fairy tale writers / [edited by] Sophie Raynard.
    p. cm.
  Includes bibliographical references and index.
  ISBN 978-1-4384-4355-3 (hardcover : alk. paper)
  ISBN 978-1-4384-4354-6 (paperback : alk. paper)
  1. Fairy tales—History and criticism.   2. Authors—Biography.   3. Children's literature, European—History and criticism.   4. Fairy tales—Authorship.
I. Raynard, Sophie.

  PN3437.T43 2012
  398.2'09—dc23
  [B]   2011048282

10 9 8 7 6 5 4 3 2 1

Contents

III
Exoticism
Galland: Eighteenth-Century France

IV
Didacticism
Jeanne-Marie Leprince de Beaumont:
Eighteenth-Century France

V
Traditionalization
Naubert: Late Eighteenth-Century and Early Nineteenth-Century Germany
The Grimms: Nineteenth-Century Germany,
Bechstein: Nineteenth-Century Germany

VI
Sentimentalization
Andersen: Nineteenth-Century Denmark

Introduction

Sophie Raynard

This book project was born from a strongly felt need to revise standard biographies of classic fairy-tale authors and editors and to present them together in a single volume. Documentary evidence, sometimes newly discovered, sometimes newly recovered from nineteenth-century suppressions, here reconfigures long-familiar images. In the case of Henriette-Julie de Castelnau, Countess de Murat, the sixteen-year-old ingénue dressed in Breton folk costume who charmed members of Louis XIV's court dissolves in the face of police evidence of a tumultuous private life, punctuated by detentions because of scandalous lesbian liaisons and physical violence. Marie-Catherine Le Jumel de Barneville, Baroness d'Aulnoy, was a fifteen year old married off to an old débauché, whom she, by the age of nineteen, tried vainly to have executed with the help of her mother and her mother's lover. And Jeanne-Marie Leprince de Beaumont, a prim and highly moral governess and author of improving books for girls, had a colorful past that included marital ambiguities. These women were all influential authors of fairy tales in the same long European tradition that included Charles Perrault, Antoine Galland, Benedikte Naubert, the Grimm brothers, and Hans Christian Andersen.

The biographies of other classic tellers of fairy tales have been unevenly available. Giovan Francesco Straparola's life was largely undocumented; Giambattista Basile's was little publicized. Others were well documented but skewed in their presentation. Perrault, for example, so often presented as a courtier, took little part in court society even though he had an office in the Versailles palace for some years. The Grimms' social lives were only examined with reference to their collection's origins in the 1980s, while Andersen's life remained until recently sentimentalized by an adoring public into a fairy tale that Andersen himself fostered.

Although scores of nineteenth-, twentieth-, and twenty-first-century editions and translations of Perrault's tales can be found today, those of his contemporaries d'Aulnoy, Bernard, Lhéritier, Murat, and de La Force, whose much larger oeuvre outshone Perrault's in the seventeenth and eighteenth centuries, largely dropped from view in the nineteenth and twentieth centuries. Consequently, earlier researchers had to resort to rare and original editions from research libraries or private collections. Moreover, reconstituting those female authors' oeuvre required, until recently, consolidating scattered tales from the novels in which many of them had been embedded. In the case of d'Aulnoy's *Contes,* Nadine Jasmin's 2004 edition marks the first time in more than two hundred years that volume 3 of her *Contes* has been printed. Similarly, the public has also rediscovered de Murat's fairy tales with Geneviève Patard's 2005 edition, while Lhéritier's original fairy-tale collection *Œuvres meslées* became newly available in Raymonde Robert's 2005 Champion edition, which also incorporated those of de La Force, Durand, and d'Auneuil. As scholars revisit and reedit classic authors' oeuvre, they have also reconstituted authors' lives and have contextualized their works.

Similarly partial or skewed biographies grew up around the figures who preceded the French storytellers. Only a few documents can be directly linked to Giovan Francesco Straparola, but richly layered studies of Renaissance writers' livelihoods, the worlds of print and publishing, and of daily life in Northern Italy in general and in Caravaggio and Venice in particular, have—taken together with evidence from his early and late writings—provided a basis for reconstructing his life. Giambattista Basile left more tracks in his world, and from them Nancy Canepa, who has newly translated Basile's *Pentamerone* into English, has created a coherent biography.

As for the storytellers who followed the French authors of the late seventeenth-century fairy-tale vogue, their biographies also appear here in newly revised form. In the case of Jeanne-Marie Leprince de Beaumont, historical detective work has fleshed out a past that de Beaumont had carefully obscured. In the case of the Grimms, the powerful historical current of nationalism long shaped Jacob and Wilhelm Grimms' biographies into exemplars of national virtues that in essential respects misleadingly embellished the lives they actually lived. Much the same thing happened with the biography of Hans Christian Andersen, whose life story was reconfigured and romanticized, while in contrast it is safe to say that few people know Ludwig Bechstein's name, and even fewer have an idea of his biography, despite the fact that his tales far outsold the Grimms' tales from the time they first appeared until the end of the nineteenth century. In short, this collection of newly researched biographies of the best-known authors of European fairy tales rectifies false data, adds new information, and provides a reliable historical context for Europe's fairy tales.

A word about the authors' names: In French we would commonly refer to women authors of the seventeenth and eighteenth centuries by their title: Mademoiselle Bernard, Mademoiselle Lhéritier, Madame de Murat, Mademoiselle de La Force, and Madame d'Aulnoy, but to men authors simply by their last name: Perrault, Galland. English usage since the 1980s requires similar forms of identification for men and women writers, and we will follow that pattern in this book. It has become customary in English to refer to Madame d'Aulnoy as d'Aulnoy even though this is not acceptable in French, but because it is common practice among English-speaking scholars we will do the same here.

I

Emergence

Straparola
Sixteenth-Century Italy

Basile
Seventeenth-Century Italy

Europe's First Fairy Tales

Ruth B. Bottigheimer

Before Giovan Francesco Straparola published the two volumes of *Le Piacevoli Notti* (*Pleasant Nights*, sometimes translated as *Facetious Nights*) in 1551 and 1553, there was no evidence of fairy tales as we know them in the modern world. That is not to say that tales with magic did not exist. In fact, they did so in large numbers as components of epic cycles such as Lodovico Ariosto's and Matteo Maria Boiardo's *Orlando* romances or those in *Amadis de Gaul*, to name only a few, along with much else that is familiar from modern fairy tales, such as quests, royalty, supernatural helpers, and wicked opponents. As in many medieval romances, the princes and princesses in these romances endured innumerable sufferings and adventures in lengthy narratives. Like later European fairy tales, their core narratives were not fixed, but could be—and often were—augmented by additional episodes that were inserted or appended.

In the later fifteenth century, romances suitable for public performance were composed, printed, performed, and sold. One such was *Lionbruno*, one of whose earliest editions was printed in Venice in 1470.[1] Popular print was a flourishing enterprise, as is evident from the rich holdings of fifteenth- and sixteenth-century publications in libraries in every western European country. Among those ancient booklets, however, there is nowhere any evidence of the brief narrative form now known as "fairy tales."

Europe's first fairy tales appeared among the seventy-some tales of Straparola's *Pleasant Nights*. Some followed a pattern that had been established in restoration plots since the writings of the ancient Greeks. Also popular in the Middle Ages, restoration stories had a prince or princess who was ousted from home and who suffered tasks and trials until restored to royal station.

Straparola regularized and abbreviated restoration tales into a recognizable fairy-tale paradigm. Different from the endless romances still being produced in the early sixteenth century, his restoration fairy tales were brief enough to be read from beginning to end at a single sitting. In terms of plot, Straparola's restoration fairy-tale heroes and heroines suffered, as did those in previous romances, but they were restored to their royal positions, specifically, by means of magic together with marriage. It is perhaps a reflection of their narrative ancestry that Straparola's restoration fairy tales were longer than his newly invented rise fairy tales. And it is possibly a refraction of the restoration heros' and heroines' high social class that they themselves tended to independently manipulate the magic at their disposal.

In the end, Straparola created a handful of restoration fairy tales, often from recognizable popular medieval components, such as saints' lives and romances. His restoration fairy tales—which thus linked medieval narratives to the modern world—were disseminated into Italy, France, Germany, and Spain, in a more than sixty-year history of repeated printings in those countries.

It is striking that Straparola's restoration tales are relatively absent from the later Neapolitan collection of his fellow Italian Giambattista Basile, while so many survived in French rewritings, principally by Charles Perrault, Marie-Catherine d'Aulnoy, and Henriette-Julie de Murat, with one living on in Antoine Galland's *Thousand and One Nights*.

Straparola's lasting contribution to the history of European fairy tales, however, is his transformation of restoration fairy-tale plots (ousted royalty suffers tasks and trials resolved by magic and marriage) into rise fairy tales by inserting a poor boy or girl into the initial cast of characters of restoration fairy tales and by foregrounding the poor protagonist's access to wealth at the end. In contrast, stories about poor individuals who became wealthy, like Dick Whittington, had heroes whose wealth preceded their marriage, rather than resulting from it, as in Straparola's new rise fairy-tale plots.

Straparola's restoration fairy tales can be seen as the product of a new assembling of traditional narrative components. The existence of a popularly performed narrative like *Lionbruno* suggests that his rise fairy tales can also be understood as a development and refinement of earlier tendencies to incorporate a poor protagonist into a popular narrative such as *Lionbruno*.

Straparola's first efforts to create a rise fairy tale were clumsy. However, his final rise fairy-tale creation "Costantino Fortunato" perfectly melded an impoverished and persecuted hero with fairy-mediated magic to achieve marriage to royalty through which the poor boy became wealthy.

It is not only in his cast of characters that Straparola's restoration and rise fairy tales differ from one another. His rise fairy tales were significantly briefer than his restoration fairy tales. In addition, his impoverished rise fairy-tale heroes and heroines did not manipulate magic to their advantage as did the royal heroes and heroines of restoration fairy tales, but they were instead often magic's unwitting beneficiaries. All of this, taken together, promotes a distinction between more active restoration heroes and heroines and less active rise heroes and heroines in Straparola's tales.

Magic was not part of the historically highly commercial, pragmatic, and worldly Republic of Venice. Hence Straparola consistently removed magic from Venice, as he did the kings and queens, princes and princesses of rise and restoration tales that are categorically alien to the Republic, where, in a delicate governmental balancing act, an elected duke governed in conjunction with a powerful senate.

Market reality similarly contributed to the content of Straparola's fairy tales. In the later Middle Ages and Renaissance, town- and city-dwelling artisans, shopkeepers, merchants, and their employees were typically literate. More than anything else, that may account for the extraordinary efflorescence, publication, and sales of story collections beginning with Boccaccio and continuing with *Les Cent Nouvelles Nouvelles (The One Hundred New Tales)* and their many subsequent imitators. Italians produced, consumed, and recycled secular stories in larger numbers than did writers in any other European country. The invention of print broadened potential book ownership by lowering book prices, and as economies expanded, rising wages enabled new social groups (such as artisans, urban craftsmen, and wage earners of both sexes) to become book and story buyers.

As folkloristic performance studies have convincingly demonstrated, performers (and we may add, writers as well) contour stories to the audiences they face. It was amid circumstances like these—a broadly literate urban public and a fluctuating Venetian economy—that Straparola composed his rise fairy tales. When the economy contracted, town and city dwelling men's and women's ability to achieve earthly comfort through their labor shrank. We may reasonably assume, however, that their appetite for wealth did not shrink, but grew when there was less food on the table and that rise fairy tales had an even greater appeal in lean times.

At the end of his life Straparola appears to have been operating within an urban milieu like that described above. The rise fairy-tale plots he invented were a perfect response to urban social conditions and aspirations. Like the Grimms, Straparola was far ahead of his day in addressing an urban proletariat, and his rough but hopeful rise fairy tales included a rough and hopeful urban audience.

Straparola had improvised a new literary form; his successor Giambattista Basile introduced a new content that became a permanent part of the European fairy-tale tradition. Like Straparola, Basile's stories were addressed to a specific audience. In his case, however, artisans do not seem to figure as a part of his intended audience; instead, everything we know about Basile's life and much that we can glean from his stories themselves suggest that he initially composed them for a privileged group of contemporaries who were knowledgeable about the arts and sciences. The also had a more than passing acquaintance with Latin classics such as Ovid's *Metamorphoses*. Given that the *Metamorphoses* were a standard part of upper-class schooling, and that Ovid's mythology was widely available in Italian translation, and that individual episodes from classical mythology were built into contemporary paintings and operas, it is not surprising that contemporary readers are able to identify large numbers of Ovidian elements in Basile's *Cunto de li cunti*, or *The Pentamerone*, as it is better known.

Two generations after their first printing (in five fascicles between 1534 and 1636), a copy of Basile's collection appears to have fallen into the hands of several French authors, Marie-Jeanne Lhéritier, her uncle Charles Perrault, and Charlotte-Rose de La Force. They all softened Basile's plots and toned down his raucous imagery, making them suitable for a more refined and distinctly less carnavalesque taste in the late seventeenth and of the dawning eighteenth century.

There were thus four steps in the emergence of fairy tales as they are known in the modern world:

1. Medieval and early modern collections of stories composed within a framing tale first provided a format for transforming earlier tale material and then recycling it to subsequent generations of readers.

2. Restoration and rise fairy-tale plot lines were developed by Straparola in Renaissance Venice.

3. Classical imagery and elements were sluiced into the new genre of brief magic tales by Basile in the Baroque period.

4. The origins of modern fairy tales were elaborated at the end of the seventeenth century, in a period in which Rococo literary style emerged from French literary classicism.

Note

1. *The Story of Lionbruno*, trans. Beatrice Corrigan (Toronto: Toronto Public Library, 1976).

Secondary Literature

Bottigheimer, Ruth B. *Fairy Godfather: Straparola, Venice, and the Fairy Tale Tradition*. Philadelphia: University of Pennsylvania Press, 2002.
———. *Fairy Tales: A New History*. Albany: State University of New York Press, 2009.
Canepa, Nancy. *From Court to Forest: Giambattista Basile's Lo cunto de li cunti and the Birth of the Literary Fairy Tale*. Detroit: Wayne State University Press, 1999.
———, trans. and ed. *Giambattista Basile's* The Tale of Tales, or Entertainment for Little Ones. Detroit: Wayne State University Press, 2007.
Rak, Michele, ed. Basile. *Lo cunto de li cunti contesto napoletano e traduzione a fronte*. Milan: Garzanti, 1998.

Giovan Francesco Straparola

1485?–1556?

Ruth B. Bottigheimer

Documentation for the life of Giovan Francesco Straparola is sparse. Two books were published under his name during his lifetime: *Opera nova* (*New Works*) of 1508, reprinted and slightly expanded in 1515, and the book by which the modern world knows him, *Le piacevoli notti* (*Pleasant Nights*). Dated 1550 by the then prevailing Julian calendar, volume 1 of the first edition of *Pleasant Nights* appeared in January 1551 (by the modern calendar), volume 2, two years later in 1553. For this collection of stories, Straparola received a ten-year copyright.[1] These few documents provide the sole currently available evidence from which a broad outline for Straparola's life can be inferred. On the title pages of both books Straparola identifies himself as coming from Caravaggio, a small town in northwestern Italy in the Duchy of Milan. No other contemporaneous document mentions his name. Since his first book was published in 1508, he was probably born in the 1480s. However, social, economic, and political conditions in northern Italy during the Renaissance extend the possible outlines of Straparola's life and suggest likely details.

Literacy rates were high in fifteenth-century urban Italy, particularly in the north. Caravaggio itself, with a population of five or six thousand, had one school for children of its highest social classes and other communal schools for the children of ordinary town-dwellers; it is virtually certain that Straparola attended one of the latter.[2] There he would have studied the standard curriculum: a commercial arithmetic of approximations ("abbaco") along with the rules of the standard literary, Florentine, Italian of his day.

Like other youngsters in communal schools, Straparola would have been exposed to the lively exemplary stories of virtue and vice in *Fior di virtù* (*Flower of Virtue*). Readings from the Bible in Italian translation would have provided a literary introduction to Christian liturgy, while the lives of the church fathers and Christian saints would have expanded his own, and other children's, knowledge of Catholic tradition. Cheap soft-covered imprints of chivalric romances would have opened a world of knightly adventure, suffering heroines, gallant heroes, and occasional magic.[3] The performance of chivalric romances by storysingers and storytellers in town squares all over northern Italy makes it safe to assume that the young Straparola knew of at least one fifteenth-century proto-fairy tale, *Lionbruno*. Published in Venice in the 1470s and designed for public performance, its text was readily available for sale to urban listeners. Straparola's later literary borrowings from Boccaccio's oeuvre show that he was well acquainted with Italy's classic and—in the Renaissance—most highly praised author.

It has been argued that Straparola was related to one of Caravaggio's leading families, the Secco, but the fact that Straparola's surname is a characterization—it means "gabby," "prolix," "garrulous," "wordy"—rather than a family name suggests that his family origins were humble,[4] as does the absence of "Straparola" as a family name in any Caravaggio records. Supporting a hypothesis of Straparola's low to middling origins is the detailed laborer's knowledge of grapevine pruning that emerges from his writings. Straparola may have been a foundling adopted into a family of modest means, a possibility corroborated by the emotional intensity in the narration of the childhood and youth of Fortunio, an orphan protagonist in one of his longer stories.

Known conditions in Caravaggio in the 1480s and 1490s provide a plausible background for Straparola's youthful years. The town bustled with construction activity, as the imposing church of San Bernardino of Siena was built. Pilgrims from beyond Caravaggio's town walls flocked to the Sanctuary of the Blessed Virgin of Caravaggio, who—decades before—had appeared to comfort a young peasant woman suffering at the hands of her violent husband. The then simple wooden structure lay outside the town walls, but the road to it from the east ran through the center of Caravaggio. A boy ranging freely in Caravaggio's streets and perhaps in the countryside round about, habits that are consistent with childrearing practices at the time, would observe artisanal crafts, the building trades, agricultural products, commercial commodities, and religious devotion. These parts of Caravaggio's public life as well as the town's social and economic conditions, even its eating habits during the 1480s, 1490s, and early 1500s are well known[5]; the extent to which the young Straparola was privy to or shared in his surroundings may be conjectured with a relatively high degree of probability.

Caravaggio's serenity and prosperity suffered at the end of the fifteenth and beginning of the sixteenth centuries, when first the French King Louis XII, then the Holy Roman Emperor Charles V, and later the French King Francis I led armies onto the Lombard plain of northern Italy to wage war, principally against the Republic of Venice. Within Caravaggio itself, alliances and overlordships shifted, and the economy weakened. Uncertainty ruled the day. But when Straparola wrote of Caravaggio in the next to last of his sonnets in the 1508 *New Works*, he addressed his birthplace intimately as a "blessed citadel" ("castel venturato").

It was probably sometime in the early 1500s that Straparola went from Caravaggio to Venice. Although transferring fictional information to historical biography can be a slippery operation, it is nonetheless useful to delve into the lives of two of Straparola's heroes, Fortunio and Zambò, because those tales might well bear a resemblance to his own life experiences. Like Straparola, Fortunio was born in (from a Venetian point of view) the most distant parts of Lombardy, which is how story 4 of night 3 of the *Pleasant Nights* describes the homeland of its hero. In a second tale, story 3 of night 5, the hero Zambò's travels suggest a route that Straparola could have taken to Venice from those western provinces. In addition, Straparola gave this tale local immediacy by having it told in dialect by Antonio Molino, a then living author who had himself composed a comic dialect piece about a laborer from Bergamo, which lies close to Caravaggio. The telling details of Zambò's journey, however, were probably Straparola's own creation. Just as the emotional intensity of Fortunio's story lends it a credible immediacy, so too does the sharp description of the hero's pair of red pigskin shoes, while the hero's disastrously ingenuous truthtelling seems more like a personal memory than an invented story element. That is above all true of the workplace accident Zambò suffered in Fusina, just across from Venice on the mainland:

> Zambò wandered around the city for a long time, and not having found work and not having a penny so that he could eat,

he was in a bad way. But after a long time, by God's grace, he came to Fusina, but because he was penniless nobody would take any interest in him, so that the poor man didn't know what to do. And seeing that the boatmen who turned the machines for drawing boats ashore earned a few farthings, he set himself to doing such work. But fate, which always persecutes the poor and the disgraced, arranged that one day when he was turning the machine, the leather strap snapped, unwound, and made a spar hit him in the chest. That threw him to the ground un-conscious, where for a time he lay stretched out like a corpse and if certain kind-hearted men hadn't hauled him into their boat by his arms and legs and rowed him back to Venice, he would have died there.

Just as no documentary evidence links Straparola to Fortunio's childhood and adolescence or to Zambò's youth, so too is there no sur-viving document between 1508 and 1551 that links Straparola to a wage-earning position, to a family, to a known quarter of Venice, or to a recognized location on the mainland. Instead, we must make do with historical possibilities and likelihoods.

We may infer Straparola's higher than usual level of literacy from the book that he published in 1508. Even though his verse is notably inferior to classic Italian writers such as Francesco Petrarch and Pietro Bembo, the fact that he published such a volume shows that he was capable of literary composition at a time when that talent was valued for its utility in a variety of salon settings. The further fact that Straparola republished his work a second time in 1515 allows us to infer that he meant it to readvertise his skills. Finally, the fact that he added only two sonnets for the 1515 printing strongly suggests that if he had worked as a poet under his own name between 1505 and 1515, he surely would have been able to add more than two sonnets to his own corpus in that period of time. As a wordsmith with no other early works under his own name, it may be inferred that Straparola had put his literary skills to work in another person's service.

Professions theoretically open to a literary man in the early six-teenth century were few. Positions in Venice's civil service were open only to *cittadini*, native-born Venetians whose families had not been tainted by physical labor for at least three generations. On the first count (birthplace) Straparola was ineligible and very likely on the second as well (parental and grandparental physical labor). As one of Venice's *popolani*, he might aspire to a nonofficial position, however, such as ones that utilized verbal skills: tutor, teacher, or private secretary. Venice's burgeoning sixteenth-century print industry is another theoretically possible place of employment, but recent research in that field has not identified Straparola among Venice's sixteenth-century "poligrafi," who earned their living working for printing or publishing houses.

A possible calling, alien to modern custom, would have been as a supplier of stories and witticisms to a frequenter of salons who had little time or talent for composing his own orally delivered contributions. Though little known in the modern world, working as a paid pen was a well-documented historical phenomenon in the Renaissance. It is also one with which the long gap between the early and late dates of Straparola's publications is persuasively consistent. Such a position was part and parcel of a patronage system that recognized and rewarded demonstrated talent. Historically, patronage has taken many forms. The most personal, and the one that Straparola is most likely to have experienced, was, as the social historian Peter Burke defined it, a "household system [in which] a rich man takes [an] artist or writer into his house for some years, gives him board, lodging, and presents, and expects to have his artistic and literary needs attended to."[6] The timing of Straparola's publications, at the beginning of a professional career, and again as a prolific producer of stories, enigmas, and songs, after the passage of several decades, is consistent with a writing career within the established Venetian patronage system.

Straparola's *Opera nova* publicly displays his talent for versifying in a number of modes and also provides internal evidence of patronage. He had named a "*miser Lafranco*" in the forward to the 1508 edition, which suggests that he hoped for patronage either from or through "milord" (*miser*). Straparola may well have found a modest patronage position before 1508, to judge from the content of his sonnets, *strambotti*, and *capitoli*: a great many recounted a desperately phrased longing for a mistress, who—remaining "cruel"—left his loving devotion unrequited.

Straparola either moved on the periphery of or knew of the lofty contemporary social literary figures with whom he peopled his invented frame tale: Ottaviano Maria Sforza (1477–1541?), the posthumously and illegitimately born son of Duke Galeazzo of Milan; Gregorio Casale (c. 1490–1536), who represented England's interests to the papacy; and Pietro Bembo (1470–1547), a prominent churchman and celebrated author. It may be significant that the acclaimed Casale and Bembo remain silent in Straparola's *Pleasant Nights* while it was men of lesser talents who joined in the storytelling: Bernardo Capello (1498–1565), who ghost-wrote for the Marquis del Vasto, and Antonio Molino (1495–1571), parts of whose Zambò story Straparola had incorporated into his own Zambò tale. Unlike the bland and categorical descriptions of Casale and Bembo, with whom Straparola might have had at best a passing acquaintance, his believable personifications of the lesser literati suggest personal acquaintance.

Straparola distinguished male storytellers in his frame tale in moral terms by placing only unambiguously worded riddles in their mouths, unlike the sexually suggestive double entendres he had his charming female storytellers utter. Such evidence internal to the *Pleasant Nights* points toward Straparola's having been familiar with male social gatherings devoted to literary play at which courtesans often formed a part.

Just as the frame tale of *Pleasant Nights* includes greater and lesser intellectual lights, so too are there two sorts of women. One group has family names and is represented as socially elevated, the most prominent of whom is Signora Lucrezia, the daughter of Ottaviano Maria Sforza. Characteristically, Straparola demonstrates confusion about this highly placed personage, however. In real life she had married a minor Gonzaga; she was not the Lucrezia Gonzaga who before her marriage to Federico II, son of Isabella d'Este, supported the eminent Italian storyteller Matteo Bandello (1485–1562), as Straparola affirms. Thus, Straparola's major frame tale figure is not an identifiable historical figure but a conflation of two different Lucrezias, both of whom were well known at that time. The frame tale's other two eminent women are identified in the *Proem* to the *Pleasant Nights* as a Signora Chiara married to Girolamo Guidiccione from Ferrara, and Signora Veronica, the widow of Santo Orbat from Crema. With family names and places of origin that locate them socially and geographically, Signora Chiara and Signora Veronica may well have once been identifiable living persons whose otherwise undocumented lives were preserved for posterity by having been incorporated into Straparola's frame tale. Whether they are accurately identified, or whether they simply offer a glimpse into Straparola's imperfect memory we cannot know. Their narrative silence and the paucity of other information about them suggest strongly that Straparola's life played out at a distance from their world.

A second group of women, young, beautiful, socially available, and differing from one another principally in hair color and height, are likely to be either Straparola's literary creations or his imagined reflections of Venice's many courtesans. The latter is the more likely possibility, since

Straparola gave none of the young women either a family name or a place of birth, both essential pieces of information in Renaissance social directories. Furthermore, in the gender-protective world of upper-class Renaissance Venice, women of quality, such as the Signore Lucrezia, Veronica, and Chiara, would never have mixed with nameless women of uncertain background and virtue. The fictive quality of the women in the frame tale therefore offers little from which we may infer anything about Straparola's life among or his knowledge of Venice's female population, except that he knew that the first socially elevated group existed and that he had some personal knowledge of women of the demimonde.

What Straparola knew when he began composing the *Pleasant Nights* is probably a fairly reliable indicator of the nature of his experiences in the thirty-six publicly undocumented years between 1515 and 1551. Formal and informal literary gatherings existed all over Europe from the Renaissance onward, and nowhere were there more literary academies, as they were often called, than in northern Italy. Baldassare Castiglione described some in *Il Cortegiano* (*The Courtier*); reference books document others in rich detail, sometimes with listings of members and places of meeting. Venice, Treviso, and Padua each had a large share of literary gatherings, and we may safely conclude that Straparola participated in them directly or vicariously.

Possible geographical locations for Straparola's life in the decades after 1515 include mainland towns. Evidence internal to the tales suggests Padua, in whose dialect he wrote the second of his two dialect tales—story 4 of night 5—about Ceccato Rabboso and his beautiful wife, Tia. Similarly, story 8 of night 13 took place just outside Padua in Noventa, while the last story of the collection, the thirteenth story of the thirteenth night, relocated the Morlini original to Padua and referred familiarly to its imposing Church of St. Anthony as the "chiesa del Santo," as Paduans themselves do to this day. Straparola equally familiarly incorporated a voyage between Venice and Padua on the River Brenta.

The March 1550 dating of Straparola's prepublication ten-year privilege (to publish and enjoy the profits from his published work) for *Pleasant Nights* makes it possible to hypothesize his composition of the collection during the previous months by calculating backwards from this date. An examination of the text of *Pleasant Nights* suggests that he initially assembled fifty stories (five each for a ten-day storytelling session). These included magic tales that he had himself composed together with urban tales borrowed from previously published works. Internal evidence further suggests that in the late summer (of probably 1549) Straparola created a frame tale within which he embedded the fifty stories. Then he added introductory songs for each day and the concluding riddling enigmas for each story.[7]

Straparola submitted the completed manuscript for the five nights of volume 1 to Venetian authorities who were responsible for granting a privilege that would protect its author from piracy, and—despite five negative votes—the privilege was granted on 8 March 1550. In the course of the following nine months, Straparola must have negotiated with booksellers and with Comin da Trino, a prominent Venetian printer, reaching an agreement to print his book during the last months of 1550, based on the fact that the printing job was completed on 2 January 1551. Since books were normally sold as a pile of unbound sheets which the buyer had bound to his specifications, his work could therefore have been put on sale as early as the next day, 3 January 1551. Straparola saw the first printing of his book sell out at a bookseller at the Sign of Santa Alvise and witnessed in the same year a second printing placed at a bookseller near San Luca at the Sign of the Diamante, in the center of the city.

Straparola was able to provide an authorial portrait for volume 2 of his book (reproduced at the beginning of this entry), perhaps a mark of his profits from the two 1551 printings. The portrait does not idealize its sitter. Instead, it shows a man with cropped hair, a trimmed beard, a wrinkled cheek, and a furrowed brow. His eyes look away from the viewer, regarding the world with hard suspicion. He does not look satisfied with his lot in life.

Indeed, all was not smooth sailing for Straparola in 1553. Between 1551 and 1553 Straparola had been publicly criticized for having stolen stories from other sources, an accusation to which he referred in the introduction to volume 2.[8] In the context of the times, plagiarism was not a legal concept, since licit authorship allowed for recasting known plots in one's own words. Thus an allegation of literary theft would stand not so much for using a plot, but for adopting the words in which another author had told the same story.

Straparola did not specify which stories had been impugned. Instead he paradoxically defended his authorship while claiming that he had written the stories down as recounted by ten young women. This statement has been cited as evidence that Straparola got the stories of *Pleasant Nights* from a female oral tradition,[9] but the majority of his tales have been identified so clearly with stories from books printed in

Venice within the previous hundred years that his claim to oral sources is unsustainable. It is, instead, the case that Straparola's "confession" that he had gotten stories from ten young women is part of a venerable European literary trope, most fully realized in Giovanni Boccaccio's *Decameron*, the most highly regarded narrative work in Renaissance Italy. It was common practice for authors to disclaim responsibility for stories, claiming rather that they had come from someone else.

However, several stories in *Pleasant Nights* cannot be previously documented, and their existence in Straparola's collection justifies calling him the inventor of two kinds of modern fairy tales. His tales of magical restoration of princes and princesses to their rightful social position have their origins in medieval romances and saints' lives, and his "Tebaldo" (story 4 of night 1) initiated a fairy-tale plot that was subsequently adopted by Giambattista Basile, Charles Perrault, and the Grimm brothers. In this tale a widowed king determines to marry his own daughter, Princess Doralice. Having failed to dissuade him, she escapes to England, serves the king as an invisible chambermaid, and marries him. Restored to royal estate, she then suffers a second round of trials, her unmagical restoration echoing episodes in the Renaissance Italian Orlando cycle.

A second kind of fairy tale in Straparola's collection was his own invention, the rise fairy tale. These tales incorporate a plot line completely new to Europe's literary tradition, one in which a poor girl or boy benefits from magical mediation to marry royalty and become wealthy. Straparola's first effort, story 1 of night 2, grafts a rise fairy-tale plot onto a restoration fairy tale about a prince suffering the effects of enchantment. In "Re Porco" ("Prince Pig") a desperately poor but beautiful girl marries a prince cursed by a mischievous fairy before conception with the habits and appearance of a pig. Suffering his embraces, the girl is astonished that he casts off his pigskin at night to reveal a handsome face and body. With his parents' help, he is restored, she eventually becomes a queen, and they live together happily ever after.

Straparola's masterpiece creation was the rise fairy tale of "Costantino Fortunato," in which a poor boy is magically helped by a fairy cat to a royal wedding and wealth. Without any trace of the restoration fairy-tale plots that linger in most of his other rise fairy tales, "Costantino Fortunato" perfectly realized the potential for rise fairy tales that has made them the most beloved fantasy form for children and adults in the modern world.

Comin da Trino published a second edition of volume 1 of the *Pleasant Nights* in 1555 and of volume 2 in 1556. Straparola had signed its foreword on 11 January, and he probably lived to see both, including book 2 with his author's portrait, on the shelves of the bookstore at the sign of Saint Alvise. The portrait's 1556 appearance was its last, just as Straparola's 11 January foreword is his last available dated communication. Comin da Trino fostered an impression of the books' continuing popularity by producing "new" printings of volume 1 in 1556 and 1557. In reality, a minute examination of the "new printings" reveals a publisher's public relations trick: in 1556 and 1557 Comin da Trino, or perhaps the bookseller at the Sign of Saint Alvise, affixed a newly dated title page to the text of the 1555 imprint of volume 1.

Subsequent, genuinely new, printings of *Pleasant Nights* do not bear Straparola's portrait. Had he still been living, he would have wished in all likelihood to continue to have an authorial portrait, since that practice confirmed an author's having achieved public success in Renaissance Italy. His portrait's absence, together with the fact that no newly dated foreword subsequently appeared, suggests that Straparola was still alive as the 1556 volume 2 with his portrait went into production, but that he died before the "1557" edition was prepared. That supposition is given further validity by the fact that plague struck Venice in the winter of 1555–56.

Straparola had achieved a certain eminence by publishing *Pleasant Nights*. Had he died in Venice, his name would have appeared in Venetian death rolls. However, that is not the case, and we must surmise that when it became clear that plague would overtake the island republic of Venice, Straparola fled to the mainland. He would have been about seventy years old in the winter of 1555–56, an advanced age at which his elderly body might have fallen prey to any number of ailments, including the ravaging plague.

Straparola did not live to see the internationalization of his stories. They were most successful in France, where they were repeatedly published in Lyons, Paris, and Rouen from 1560 to 1615. In the same period *Pleasant Nights* was published in Germany on three recorded occasions—1575, 1582, and 1590—as well as in Spain. Only one of Straparola's fairy tales was reprinted in England, "Dionigi" ("The Tailor's Apprentice," story 4, [sometimes numbered story 5] of night 8), in chapbook form. After the French fairy-tale vogue at the turn of the eighteenth century, *Pleasant Nights* was published in Amsterdam (1725) and Paris (1726).

Notes

1. Register of the Archivio di Stato di Venezia Senato Terra, filza 37, carta 4v, as cited by Donato Pirovano, 1: liii.

2. Santagiuliana, 100.

3. Bottigheimer, 49–51. For a discussion of northern Italian schooling in the Renaissance see Grendler.

4. Both A. Mazzi and Ann Motte favor a connection between the Secco and Straparola. See Bottigheimer, 134, note 5.

5. Santagiuliana covers all of these subjects in his study, and I include them in chapter 3 of *Fairy Godfather*.

6. Burke, *The Italian Renaissance*, 114.

7. For a detailed discussion underlying these statements see Bottigheimer, *Fairy Godfather*, 82–119.

8. For the text of this preface, see *Fairy Tales Framed: Early Forewords, Afterwords, and Critical Words* (Albany: State University of New York Press, 2012).

9. Klotz, 34.

Giovan Francesco Straparola's Works

Verse

Opera nova de Zoan Francesco Straparola da Caravazo, novamente stampata: Sonetti cxv, Strambotti xxxv, Epistole vii, Capitoli xii. Venice: Georgio de Ruschoni, 1508.

Opera nova de Zoan Francesco Straparola da Caravazo, novamente stampata: Sonetti cxvii, Strambotti xxxv, Epistole vii, Capitoli xii. Venice: Alexandro di Bindoni, 1515.

Le piacevoli Notti di M. Giovan Francesco Straparola da Caravaggio. Nelle qvali si contengono le fauole con i loro enimmi da dieci donne, & duo giouani raccontate, cosa diletteuole ne piu data in luce [vol. 1]. Venice: [Printed by Comin da Trino di Monferatto for] Orpheo dalla carta tien per insegna S. Aluise, 1550 [=1551].

Le piacevoli Notti di M. Giovanfrancesco Straparola da Caravaggio. Nelle qvali si contengono le fauole con e lor (sic) enigmi da dieci donne raccontate, cosa diletteuole ne piu data in luce [Volume 2]. Venice: [Printed by Comin Trino di Monferatto for] San Bartholameo alla libraria della colombina, 1553.

The Facetious Nights of Giovanni Francesco Straparola da Caravaggio. Trans. W. G. Waters, illus. Jules Garnier and E. R. Hughes. 4 vols. London: Society of Bibliophiles, 1898 [English edition]. N.B. A new translation by Suzanne Magnanini is in progress and will soon be published.

Le Piacevoli Notti, ed. Donato Pirovano. Rome: Salerno Editrice, 2000 [critical edition].

Secondary Literature

Bottigheimer, Ruth B. *Fairy Godfather: Straparola, Venice, and the Fairy Tale Tradition*. Philadelphia: University of Pennsylvania Press, 2002.

Burke, Peter. *The Italian Renaissance: Culture and Society in Italy*. Princeton: Princeton University Press, 1986.

Castiglione, Baldassar. *The Book of the Courtier*. Trans. Leonard Eckstein Opdyke. New York: Charles Scribner's Sons, 1903.

Grendler, Paul. *Schooling in Renaissance Italy: Literacy and Learning, 1300–1600*. Baltimore: Johns Hopkins Press, 1989.

———. "Chivalric Romances in the Italian Renaissance." *Studies in Medieval and Renaissance History* 10 (1998): 57–102.

———. "What Piero Learned in School: Fifteenth-Century Vernacular Education." In *Piero della Francesca and His Legacy*, ed. Marilyn Aronberg Lavin. Washington: National Gallery of Art, 1995. 161–76.

Klotz, Volker. *Das Europäische Kunstmärchen. Fünfundzwanzig Kapitel seiner Geschite von der Renaissance bis zur Moderne*. Stuttgart: Verlagsbuchhandlung, 1985.

Pirovano, Donato. "Una storia editoriale cinquecentesca: 'Le piacevoli notti' di Giovan Francesco Straparola." *Giornale storico della letterature italiana* 177 (2000): 540–69.

———. "Per l'edizione de *Le Piacevoli Notti* di Giovan Francesco Straparola." *Filologia Critica* 26 (2001): 60–93 [listing of libraries holding the original editions of *Piacevoli Notti*].

Rua, Giuseppe. "Intorno alle 'Piacevoli Notti' dello Straparola." *Giornale storico della letteratura italiana* 15 (1890): 111–51.

———. "Intorno alle 'Piacevoli Notti' dello Straparola." *Giornale storico della letteratura italiana* 16 (1890): 218–83.

———. *Le «piacevoli notti» die Messer Gian Francesco Straparola: Ricerche di Giuseppe Rua*. Rome: Loescher, 1898.

Santagiuliana, Tullio. *Caravaggio: Profilo storico*. Treviglio: Signorelli, 1981.

Giambattista Basile

1575?–1632

Nancy Canepa

Giambattista Basile led an active and itinerant life as a man of letters, soldier, and administrator, a life that was in many ways typical for a seventeenth-century courtier. But Basile's literary persona was two sided. On the one hand, there is the large corpus of Italian works written in the style of his contemporary Giambattista Marino, the great Baroque poet, many of which were occasional pieces produced on command for the local prince or noble on whom he depended for financial support. Basile, a meticulous philologist, produced editions of several major late Renaissance poets and belonged to a number of literary academies, actively participating in the cultural debates that took place there.

Basile also wrote in his native Neapolitan dialect. It is for these works that he is remembered today: a series of jocose letters and the nine-part *Muse napoletane* (The Neapolitan Muses), verse eclogues that depict aspects of popular culture in Naples, such as "Clio, or the Swashbucklers," "Euterpe, or the Courtesan," and "Calliope, or Music." His dialect masterpiece is *Lo Cunto de li cunti overo lo trattenemiento de' peccerille* (The Tale of Tales or Entertainment for Little Ones; or as it is better known, *The Pentamerone*), a collection of fifty fairy tales.

Basile was born to Cornelia Daniele and her husband, of whom we know only the surname, Basile,[1] in or around 1575, just outside Naples in the village of Posillipo. Basile was one of many, perhaps seven, brothers and sisters; the family was "respectable although not well-to-do," most likely of the Neapolitan middle class that had been expanding in size throughout the sixteenth century.[2] Giambattista, as did virtually all of his siblings, spent his professional life in service at courts in Italy and abroad, and although he frequently expressed dissatisfaction at being a court intellectual, he also reaped its benefits, since by the end of his life, he had achieved substantial recognition for his literary works.

Very little is known about Basile's life before 1608. In the complete absence of documentary evidence, scholars have depended on autobiographical references within his works. These indicate that around 1600, if not before, Basile left Naples, which, with its population of two hundred thousand, was one of the largest and most animated cities of Europe and a major cultural center of the Italian Baroque. Basile sought his fortune elsewhere, as his literary efforts had evoked little interest in his native city, and he had had no success in finding a noble protector. He expressed bitterness and a sense of betrayal at his departure as well as disorientation on his later return, in his 1611 *Le Avventurose dissaventure* (The Adventurous Misadventures). In a scene set in Naples, the autobiographical character Nifeo explains to another character:

> You will hear, then, that I first opened my eyes to daylight on this very shore. It should cause no marvel that I am not recognized as a countryman here, for I have roamed afar for so long that my dress and manners appear different from those here. [. . .] When I had journeyed half of my life's way, a new spirit inflamed in me the desire for higher study, and although I knew I was a swamp bird, I strove to equal the noblest swans. But when I thought most surely that my fatherland was going to confirm me in winning laurels, I then saw that those who should have loved me most ignored me. (Ah, the harsh conditions of our age, in which the noblest virtues of children are abhorred by their own mothers.) And so I arranged to flee the ungrateful shores, and to search for my fortune elsewhere.[3]

After a number of intermediate stops (we know neither where nor when) Basile ended up in Venice. There he enlisted as a soldier of fortune and was soon afterward sent to Crete, then called "Candia," a Venetian outpost and strategic point of defense against the Turks.[4] There he served under, and entered the graces of, the Venetian nobleman Andrea Cornaro, who invited him to become a member of his

Accademia degli Stravaganti (Academy of the Eccentrics), his debut in literary society. His membership offered him experiences that would subsequently prove precious to him, such as "the association with a liminal civilized society that was composite and plurilingual, in a certain sense structurally similar to Neapolitan society, and the source of much material [. . .] that would later be used in Lo Cunto."[5]

In 1607 Basile took part in a naval battle off Corfu under the command of Giovanni Bembo, and the same year he returned to Italy with Bembo. By 1608 he was back in Naples, where he finally managed to get a foothold in literary circles, probably due to the fact that his sister Adriana, a singer, was well on her way to becoming one of the most celebrated divas of the early seventeenth century. With her fame came connections and influence. For instance, when Basile returned to Naples, she and her husband, Muzio Barone, were members of the court of Luigi Carafa, prince of Stigliano. Adriana was energetic in seeing that her brother's talents were appreciated. In Naples, Basile continued to exercise the profession of courtier, performing duties such as writing songs, devices, anagrams, and occasional verse for celebrations of significant events in the lives of his patrons. His profession also entailed organizing festivities and spectacles of every sort as well as undertaking administrative and secretarial tasks.[6]

The first known works by Basile are three letters in Neapolitan, dated 1604, which were followed by several others. In 1612 these, and subsequent letters, together with a dedication "A lo re de li viente" ("To the King of the Winds"), were published as the preface to Giulio Cesare Cortese's mock-epic Neapolitan poem, La Vaiasseide (The Epic of the Servant Girls), for which Basile also wrote thematic summaries preceding each canto. Basile's letters reveal characteristics that would mark his later dialect writings, such as "the calculated antinomy of literary Neapolitan to literary Tuscan and its traditions; [. . .] the attention to forms of narrative inspired by non-literary models; [. . .] the perception of the literary effects that could be obtained through the contamination of texts, genres, and discourses deriving from different cultural areas and registers."[7] Here Basile also used for the first time the anagrammatic pseudonym with which he later signed all of his Neapolitan works: Gian Alessio Abbattutis (abbattuto means dejected or depressed).

Apart from a single villanella[8] in a 1605 verse collection, Basile's first work in standard Italian was published in 1608 (although it was probably written in Crete). This was the short poem Il Pianto della vergine (The Tears of the Virgin), modeled on the late-sixteenth-century

Neapolitan poet Luigi Tansillo's *Lagrime di San Pietro*. In the same year he composed a number of courtly panegyrics, one of which celebrated the marriage of Cosimo dei Medici to Mary Magdalene of Austria.[9] The first edition of *Madriali et ode* (Madrigals and Odes) was published in 1609. It was a volume of limited literary interest that nevertheless constituted another milestone in his literary career.[10]

In early 1610, when Vincenzo Gonzaga, duke of Mantua, invited Adriana to join his court, she stipulated that her husband and brother (Giambattista) must be hired along with her. The duke accepted her conditions, and in May Adriana and Muzio (but not Giambattista) left for Mantua. Benedetto Croce suggests that Basile chose not to go (although he did join his sister later), because he hoped to take over Muzio's position and prestige in the Stigliano court, where he was already serving. In 1610, in fact, Basile dedicated to Carafa (prince of Stigliano) a marine pastoral set in Posillipo, *Le Avventurose disavventure* (The Adventurous Misadventures), published the following year. This genre, a variation on the ever-popular pastoral (in which shepherds become fishermen, nymphs, mermaids, and so forth) was in vogue, especially in Naples. Croce describes Basile's version as "one of the usual maritime tales with the usual kidnapping by Turks [. . .] stories of characters who fall in love with the wrong person, a woman who wanders through the world dressed as a man, commonplaces of the lovesick shepherd or fisherman, laments against Fortune's caprices, and concluding recognitions and marriages."[11]

Many of the pastoral motifs are shared by the fairy tale. And indeed, although on the surface Basile's works in dialect and those in Tuscan seem to be distinct areas of literary activity, they are frequently interdependent. Moreover, the choice of marine pastoral involved an attempt to rewrite a conventional genre in a distinctly Neapolitan key, an enterprise that not only allowed for a "native" space of literary creativity but also aggressively promoted local historical identity and popular cultural heritages, all of which would later be expressed exhaustively and spectacularly in *The Pentamerone*.[12]

In 1611 Basile became a founding member of the Neapolitan Accademia degli Oziosi (Academy of the Idle). Officially instituted by the Marquis of Villa, Giambattista Manso, it was one of the most important academies of its day and a crossroads of Italian and Spanish culture. For instance, the prominent Spanish poet Francisco de Quevedo (1580–1645) was a member during the years he spent in Naples. Basile's personal device was a snail at the foot of a mountain, and his academic name, "Il Pigro" ("The Lazy"), remained the same as the one he had used among the Eccentrics in Crete. In 1612 were published the *Egloghe amorose e lugubri* (*Amorous and Lugubrious Eclogues*), a musical drama *Venere addolorata* (Venus Afflicted), and several occasional pieces composed for marriages and deaths of members of the Mantuan court. Later in 1612 Basile traveled to Mantua to join his sister, who had by this time acquired an estate from the Gonzaga ruler. In 1613 Basile, too, received the favors of the new duke Ferdinando, who named him one of his court gentlemen.

Basile also continued to publish; the *Opere poetiche* (Poetic Works) of 1613 contained reeditions of most of Basile's works of 1608–12.[13] By the end of 1613 Basile was back in Naples, and in subsequent years he served as feudal administrator for various landed nobles of the Kingdom of Naples: in 1615 he was in Montemarano (province of Avellino); in 1617 in Zuncoli, under the Marquis of Trevico, Cecco di Loffredo; in 1618 with the prince of Avellino, Marino Caracciolo; and in 1619 he was named governor of Avellino. Although these were prize positions for someone like Basile, a life of continuous changes of residence and allegiance must have been tiring. We can surmise that much of the anti-court sentiment that permeates *The Pentamerone* and the other dialect works was based on experiences accumulated during these years. Indeed, Basile had already declared his profound disillusionment with court life in 1612 in the facetious dedication ("A lo re de li viente") that was included with his friend Giulio Cesare Cortese's *La Vaiasseide* (The Epic of the Servant Girls), one of the most important works of the nascent dialect tradition:

> It would be a good idea never to publish anything, but if this mistake really has to be made, my view is that the dedication should be to the wind. He must, indeed, be the greatest man in the world, for I hear him mentioned by everyone, who all say they work for him. Just look at those who serve in the courts: you serve now, you serve later, you serve today, you serve tomorrow [. . .] and then, suddenly, it's night for you, you're told to turn yourself around and get out! You can truly say that you've served the wind, and God only knows how many of those fellows there are who, instead of awarding you satisfaction, at the last minute send you away with an accusation of theft. The lover paces the floor, coughs, sneezes, runs, perspires, pines away, swells up with emotion, and when he expects at least a wink of

the eye from his coy sweetheart, he finds that he has labored in vain, for the wind! [. . .] And so the poor poet—sonnets over here, verses of every other sort over there, madrigals for this one and *barzellette* for that one—as soon as he collects his wits he finds himself with an empty head, a shrunken stomach, and ragged elbows, one foot sunk in misery, [. . .] and always naked as a louse. Everything he does goes to the wind, just as my own affairs have.[14]

At this time Basile also embarked on philological editions of a number of classic texts of the sixteenth-century Petrarchan and mannerist lyric traditions. Besides being another of the rites of passage into literary society, an endeavor of this sort had the very practical purpose of enriching Basile's own literary activity, for the formulas adopted in encomiastic works and especially verse destined to be put to music still relied, in Basile's time, on these traditions as their principal source of inspiration. In 1616 he published, in Naples, an edition of Pietro Bembo's *Rime* (Rhymes), which was followed shortly after by ancillary works on the same poet. Straparola had also drawn on Bembo by inserting him into the cast of characters in the *Pleasant Nights* frame tale. In 1617 and 1618 Basile directed his efforts to the poets Giovanni della Casa and Galeazzo di Tarsia.[15] The intensive cataloguing evidenced in these philological works was paralleled by, and perhaps preparatory to, the cataloguing of popular material that underlay Basile's two major dialect works, *The Pentamerone* and *The Neapolitan Muses*, on which Basile had probably started working as early as 1615 and that he may have read to friends and colleagues in the Neapolitan academies.[16]

The third part of Basile's *Madrigals and Odes* came out in 1617, and in this period—around 1615—Basile may have held a series of lessons on Petrarch at the Accademia degli Oziosi.[17] In 1619 Basile published *Aretusa* (Arethusa), a pastoral idyll dedicated to his employer of the moment, Marino Caracciolo. In 1620 he returned to Naples from Avellino, and in this same year he wrote the musical drama *Il Guerriero amante* (The Warrior Lover) specifically for performance by his sister Adriana, who was by this time a coveted national star. It was through her intercession with the Spanish viceroy in Naples Antonio Alvarez de Toledo (the duke of Alba) that Basile, after serving for a couple of years (1621–22) as royal governor of Lagolibero in the Basilicata region acquired the far more prestigious position as governor of Anversa in 1626. There is some evidence that *Canzoniere* (Songs) composed in

Italian and Spanish at the Accademia degli Oziosi during the years of the duke of Alba's reign (1622–29) should be attributed to Basile.[18] In 1621 the Accademia degli Incauti (Academy of the Imprudent) opened in Naples, and Basile became a member.

In 1624 Basile published *Immagini delle più belle dame napoletane ritratte da' loro propri nomi in tanti anagrammi* (Images of the Most Beautiful Neapolitan Ladies, Portrayed by their Own Names in Anagram), in which he demonstrated the penchant for enigmas and combinatory games that would be evident in *The Pentamerone* as well. He appeared on the frontispiece of this work, for the first time, as "Count of Torone" (a town in the province of Caserta), a designation that appeared in all his subsequent works and that signaled his entrance into the titled bourgeoisie. In 1627 fifty more *Odes*, dedicated to the duke of Alba, came out, and in these years Basile authored many poems in Latin, Spanish, and Italian that were used in court spectacles. One of Basile's last works was the masquerade entitled *Monte di Parnaso* (Mount Parnassus, 1630), composed for the visit to Naples of Marie of Austria, sister to the Spanish King Philip IV. Set to music by Giacinto Lombardo, it was one of the first musical dramas performed in Naples.[19] In the final period of his life Basile wrote *Del Teagene* (On Theagenes), published posthumously in 1637. A version of Heliodorus' *Aethiopica*, it—and Greek romance in general—shares many structural elements with the fairy tale. Here, too, we should note the connection with the ongoing elaboration of *The Pentamerone*.

The last court at which Basile served was that of the duke of Acerenza, Galeazzo Pinelli, a man of letters and member of the Accademia degli Oziosi. In 1631 Pinelli named Basile governor of Giugliano in the province of Naples. Basile held the post only briefly. After the 1631 eruption of Mount Vesuvius, a flu epidemic, so severe in its effects that many compared it to the plague, hit Naples and the surrounding areas. Basile, one of its victims, died on 23 February 1632 and was buried with an elaborate funeral in Giugliano's Santa Sofia church.

In 1637, a biography in *Glorie degli Incogniti* (*Glories of the Unknowns*), published by the Venetian Accademia degli Incogniti (Academy of the Unknowns), provided rare documentation of Basile's life by a contemporary:

> After he had applied himself, in the flower of his youth, to chivalrous pursuits just as much as to the study of the choicest letters, he became the true epitome of an exquisitely refined

gentleman. Along with the knowledge of the noblest disciplines, he also learned several languages. [. . .] The literary merits of Giovan Battista were rendered more worthy of respect by his eminently courteous manners, by the sincere affection that he showed toward his friends, and by his perpetual cheerfulness of spirit, for which he was deemed the life of conversations. And so he conquered not only the affection of the gentlemen and ladies [whose company] he frequented in private, but also the grace of the most exalted, who held him quite dear. And although fortune did not fail to test him by acquainting him with the hostility that she often declares to great minds, keeping him constantly distracted in troublesome occupations, he never lost heart. Up to his last breath he maintained a very peaceful tenor of life, since at the time that death took him from the living he was nourishing substantial hopes.[20]

Although this description does not paint a vivid picture of Basile as an individual, it does suggest a man who, despite his "laborious occupations," yearned for a more peaceful dimension in which his "cheerful spirit" could have full rein—a dimension that, perhaps, he was able to create only within the pages of The Pentamerone.

After Basile's death, Adriana was instrumental in getting On Theagenes published and probably also arranged for the publication of The Neapolitan Muses (1635) and The Pentamerone (1634–36).[21] We might wonder at Basile's lack of editorial self-promotion with regard to the dialect works, considering his otherwise meticulous management of his literary affairs. Perhaps he did not deem them appropriate for publication, or, possibly, there was simply less need for broad distribution, since the public for dialect literature was composed above all of select members of a single linguistic community. In Basile's case this "community" consisted of the small courts at which he served, as well as the Neapolitan academies of which he was a member. Indeed, the preferred mode of consuming a work such as The Pentamerone was in an oral setting, in the context of "courtly conversation."[22]

Basile's works in standard Italian, so well-received during his own life, ceased to be republished shortly after his death, and by the end of the seventeenth century they had fallen into oblivion. However, the popularity of The Pentamerone, on the other hand, has through the centuries steadily increased. It was initially published as five separate volumes: the first and second days in 1634 by the Neapolitan press of Ottavio

Beltrano; the third in 1634 by Lazzaro Scorriggio, also of Naples; the fourth in 1635 by Scorriggio; and the fifth in 1636, again by Beltrano. There is no trace or any mention in early biographical material on Basile of a manuscript, and thus little is known about the time or modality of composition of *The Pentamerone*.

The Pentamerone significantly influenced later fairy-tale authors with its early versions of many of what we consider today to be the classic fairy tales: "Puss in Boots," "Cinderella," "Rapunzel," and "Sleeping Beauty." The tales of *The Pentamerone* are contained by a frame (the fiftieth tale, or the "tale of the tales"), itself also a fairy tale, in which a princess named Zoza is cheated out of her predestined prince, Tadeo, by a slave girl (the "false bride" motif), to which Zoza reacts by using a magic doll to instill in the slave a craving for tales. The prince summons the "most skilled and gossipy" tale tellers in the city—a motley group of hags—and they each tell one tale apiece for five days, at the end of which Zoza tells her own story, thus revealing the slave's deceit, and winning back Tadeo. The tale telling of each day is preceded by a banquet, games, and other entertainment; verse dialogues ("Eclogues") that satirize the social ills of Basile's time follow the tales of days 1–4. In many ways the structure of Basile's work mirrors, often parodically, that of earlier novella collections, in particular Boccaccio's *Decameron*.

The interest in popular culture and folk traditions that existed in the early seventeenth century came to a spectacular culmination in *The Pentamerone*. But Basile went far beyond merely transcribing and ordering existing materials; he transformed them into thoroughly unique tales in which, in the words of one of Basile's most attentive nineteenth-century commentators, Vittorio Imbriani, "he was able to reconcile two things that would seem impossible to reconcile, above all stylistically: a distinct personality and the impersonality of the popular."[23] In Basile's richly textured narrative we find the rhetorical pyrotechnics so beloved by the baroque aesthetic, especially in the forms of extravagant metaphor, elaborate descriptions, and pastiches of materials and languages borrowed from diverse genres of popular and learned culture; encyclopedic references to the customs, everyday rituals, and popular art forms of seventeenth-century Naples; and a subtext of barbed critique of courtly culture and the canonical literary tradition. Notable thematic characteristics include the celebration of the inevitable force of love, youth, and sexual vitality, which often triumph absolutely over token obstacles ("Petrosinella," 2.1); the presentation, in many tales, of a morally indeterminate world in which cruelty, violence, and deception are winning strategies ("The Cinderella Cat," 1.6), or in which happy endings are questioned ("The Old Woman Who Was Skinned," 1.10); and a surprising number of ingenious heroines who use their intelligence instead of magic ("Sapia," 5.6). Readers of *The Pentamerone* are constantly challenged to reevaluate assumptions about fairy tales, narrative closure, moral "truths," and, in general, the viability of linguistic, cultural, and epistemological conventions and hierarchies. Above all, *The Pentamerone* constitutes a new narrative model that is one of the most complex tributes to the power of the fairy tale not only to entertain, but also to interpret the world.

Notes

1. Giorgio Fulco has argued for an earlier date of birth—1570 or 1572—according to calculations based on autobiographical sections of *Le Avventurose dissaventure* (404–5).

2. Croce, "Giambattista Basile e il *Cunto de li cunti*," 4. The biographical information included in this section is based principally on the studies by Croce (1891), Imbriani, Rak (1986), and Nigro (1979). Fulco focuses on only several moments of Basile's life and work. See Ademollo for information on the Basile family, especially Adriana, though Giambattista himself appears rarely.

3. Fulco, 402. Fulco cites another passage from this work (in 2.5) in which the same character evokes the "eighteen years" that have passed "since I, the wanderer, left my native land" in support of his claim that Basile was absent from Naples from 1590 to 1608.

4. Fulco hypothesizes that the dates of Basile's stay in Candia were 1604 through 1607.

5. Rak, *Lo Cunto*, 1048.

6. Ibid., *Napoli gentile*, 359.

7. Ibid., *Lo Cunto*, 1048.

8. Name of a type of musical or poetic composition.

9. See Rak, *Lo Cunto*, 1046–53, for a complete list of all Basile's published works, including single poems and other short compositions (*villanelle*, *canzonette*, etc.)

10. Rak notes how the choice of these two genres corresponds to Basile's principal poles of activity at this time: celebration of persons and occasions of note (*Ode*) and his involvement with music, through his sister Adriana (*Madriali*). He also hypothesizes that musical scores originally accompanied the text but were subsequently lost (*Lo Cunto*, 1050).

11. Croce, "Giambattista Basile e il *Cunto*," 11.

12. Rak, *La Maschera*, 65. Rak's analysis of Basile's Italian opus frequently articulates the thematic and structural similarities between these and the dialect works.

13. A number of letters from Basile, primarily to members of the Gonzaga family, were published by Croce (1891; the letters date 1613, 1613, 1615, and 1626) and Fulco (1611, 1612, 1615), but offer little useful biographical information.

14. Basile, *Lo Cunto . . .* , ed. Petrini 575–76. Another acid depiction of court life can be found in the eclogue "La coppella," as well as in a number of the tales themselves (e.g., 3.7, "Corvetto").

15. See Rak for complete titles (*Lo Cunto*, ed., 1051).

16. See Croce, "Giambattista Basile e il *Cunto*," 43, for supporting evidence.

17. Fulco, 387.

18. Ibid., 396.

19. Croce, "Giambattista Basile e il *Cunto*," 21.

20. Cit. Imbriani, 36–37.

21. Croce maintains that Basile had intended for *Le Muse* to be published immediately after G. C. Cortese's death in 1627, in order to fill the ensuing void in the world of dialect literature, as he himself states in the foreword to *Le Muse* ("Giambattista Basile e il *Cunto*," 44).

22. Rak, *Lo Cunto*, 1057.

23. Imbriani, 448.

Giambattista Basile's Works

Italian

Il Pianto della vergine (1608): sacred poem.

Madriali et ode (1609): verse. (Other editions of madrigals and odes were published in 1612, 1617, and 1627.)

Le Avventurose disavventure (1611): a marine pastoral drama.

Egloghe amorose e lugubri (1612): verse.

Venere addolorata (1612): a musical drama.

[*Opere poetiche* (1613): verse.]

Rime di M. Pietro Bembo (1616): edition.

Rime di M. Giovanni della Casa (1617): edition.

Rime di Galeazzo di Tarsi (1617): edition.

Aretusa (1619): a pastoral idyll.

Il Guerriero amante (1620): musical drama.

Immagini delle più belle dame [. . .] (1624); anagrammatic verse.

Monte Parnasso (1630): musical drama.
Del Teagene (1637): romance in verse (from Heliodorus' *Aethiopica*).

Neapolitan

Lettere (1612): correspondence.
Le Muse napoletane (1635): verse dialogues.
Lo Cunto de li cunti overo lo trattenemiento de' peccerille (1634–36): fairy tales.

Secondary Literature

Ademollo, A. *La Bell'Adriana*. Città di Castello: S. Lapi, 1888.

Asor Rosa, Alberto. "La Narrativa italiana del Seicento." *Le Forme del testo. La prosa*. Vol. 3, part 2 of *Letteratura italiana*. Gen. ed. Alberto Asor Rosa. Turin: Einaudi, 1984.

Calvino, Italo. "La Mappa delle metafore." *Sulla fiaba*. Turin: Einaudi, 1988.

Canepa, Nancy L. *From Court to Forest: Giambattista Basile's Lo Cunto de li cunti and the Birth of the Literary Fairy Tale*. Detroit: Wayne State University Press, 1999.

———. "Entertainment for Little Ones?" Basile's *Lo Cunto de li cunti* and the Childhood of the Literary Fairy Tale." *Marvels & Tales* 17, no. 1 (2003): 37–54.

———. trans. and ed. *Giambattista Basile's The Tale of Tales, or Entertainment for Little Ones*. Detroit: Wayne State University Press, 2007.

Calabrese, Stefano. "La Favola del linguaggio: il 'come se' del Pentamerone." *Lingua e stile* 16 (1981): 13–34.

———. "L'Enigma del racconto: Dallo Straparola al Basile." *Lingua e stile* 18 (1983): 177–98.

Croce, Benedetto, ed. and introd. *Lo Cunto de li cunti*. By Giambattista Basile: Biblioteca Napoletana di Storia e Letteratura, 1891 (republished with minor changes in *Saggi sulla letteratura italiana del Seicento*. Bari: Laterza, 1911).

———. "Giambattista Basile e il Cunto de li cunti." *Saggi sulla letteratura italiana del Seicento*. Bari: Laterza, 1911.

———. "Giambattista Basile e l'elaborazione artistica delle fiabe popolari." In Giambattista Basile, *Il Pentamerone*. Ed. and trans. Benedetto Croce. Bari: Laterza, 1982 [1925].

Fulco, Giorgio. "Verifiche per Basile: Materiali autobiografici e restauro di una testimonianza autobiografica." *Filologia e critica* 10, nos. 2–3 (1985): 372–406.

Getto, Giovanni. "La Fiaba di Giambattista Basile." *Barocco in prosa e poesia*. Milan: Rizzoli, 1969.

Glorie degl'Incogniti, overo gli huomini illustri dell'Accadema de' Signori Incogniti di Venetia. Venice, 1637. [short biography—cited in the text of the entry—and a sketch of Basile]

Guaragnella, Pasquale. "Universo fiabesco e razionalità scientifica. Temi per una lettura del Pentamerone di Giambattista Basile." In Polifonie. Soggetto e scrittura, desiderio e devianze, moda e fiaba, ed. A. Ponzio, et al. Bari: Adriatica, 1982.

———. " 'Comme [. . .]'n autro Eracleto non se vedeva maie ridere.' Malinconie e follie allo specchio ne Lo Cunto de li cunti." Le Maschere di Democrito e di Eraclito. Scritture e malinconie tra Cinque e Seicento. Fasano: Schena, 1990.

Imbriani, Vittorio. "Il Gran Basile. Studio biografico e bibliografico." Giornale Napoletano di Filosofia e Lettere, Scienze morali epolitiche 1 (1875): 23–35; 2 (1875): 194–219, 335–66, 413–59.

Nigro, Salvatore S. "Dalla lingua al dialetto: La letteratura popolaresca." In I poeti giocosi dell'età barocca, ed. Salvatore S. Nigro and Alberto Asor Rosa. Bari: Laterza, 1979.

———. "Lo Cunto de li cunti di Giovan Battista Basile." In Dal Cinquecento al Settecento. Vol. 2 of Letteratura italiana. Le Opere. Turin: Einaudi, 1993. 867–91.

Penzer, Norman, ed. and trans. The "Pentamerone" of Giambattista Basile. 2 vols. London: John Lane and the Bodley Head, 1932. Note: Penzer translation into English of Croce's translation into Italian from Neapolitan has been the standard for two generations. Nancy Canepa's new translation Giambattista Basile's The Tale of Tales, or Entertainment for Little Ones appeared with Wayne State University Press in 2007.

Petrini, Mario. Il Gran Basile. Rome: Bulzoni, 1989.

Picone, Michelangelo, and Alfred Messerli, eds. Giovan Battista Basile e l'invenzione della fiaba. Ravenna: Longo, 2004.

Porcelli, Bruno. "Il Senso del molteplice nel Pentamerone." In Novellieri italiani dal Sacchetti al Basile. Ravenna: Longo, 1969.

Rak, Michele. La Maschera della fortuna. Letture del Basile toscano. Naples: Liguori, 1975.

———. "Fonti e lettori nel Cunto de li cunti di G.B. Basile." In Tutto è fiaba, ed. Alberto M. Cirese. Milan: Emme Edizioni, 1980.

———. Napoli gentile. "La Letteratura in lingua napoletana" nella cultura barocca (1596–1632). Bologna: Il Mulino, 1994.

———, ed. and trans. Lo Cunto de li cunti by Giambattista Basile. Milan: Garzanti, 1986.

Schenda, Rudolf. "Giambattista Basile, Neapel und die mediterranen Erzähltraditionen: Ein Meer ohne Märchenhaftigkeit." Fabula 40.1–2 (1999): 33–49.

II

Elaboration

Perrault and the *Conteuses Précieuses*
Seventeenth-Century France

Sophistication and Modernization of the Fairy Tale

1690–1709

Nadine Jasmin
(translated and adapted by Sophie Raynard)

The 1690s are known in literature as the dazzling first period of the fairy-tale vogue. There have been, however, two distinct histories of this period. For nearly two centuries—from the early 1800s until the late 1900s, Charles Perrault's *Histoires, ou Contes du temps passé* (Histories, or Tales of Past Times)—occupied center stage, their content analyzed and interpreted and their author honored. In this history Perrault's brilliant achievement obscured the other history, namely, that Perrault was one writer among many creators of fairy and fairyland magic in those years. For instance, 1690 brought Marie-Catherine d'Aulnoy's tale about fairyland, "L'Ile de la félicité" ("The Island of Happiness"), 1694 Perrault's fairy tale "Peau d'Ane" ("Donkey Skin"), 1695 brought his manuscript collection "Contes de ma mère l'Oye" ("Tales of Mother Goose") for Elisabeth-Charlotte d'Orléans and Mademoiselle Lhéritier's *Oeuvres mêlées* (*Various Works*) with its fairy tales. The golden years of the first generation of French fairy tales were 1697 and 1698, with the publication of dozens of marvelous tales by Perrault and the *conteuses précieuses*.[1]

One of the essential characteristics of the 1690s production is its largely feminine dimension, since it is to the pen of seven women

41

fairy-tale writers—Marie-Catherine d'Aulnoy, Marie-Jeanne Lhéritier, Henriette-Julie de Murat, Catherine Bernard, Louise d'Auneuil, Charlotte-Rose de La Force, and Catherine Durand—that we owe more than sixty of the ninety tales published in those years. (Marc Soriano characterized d'Auneuil's output not as fairy tales but as "anti-Märchen.")[2] Durand's fairy tales had little subsequent resonance, as was also the case with Louis, Chevalier de Mailly (?–1724); Jean de Préchac (1676–?); Paul-François Nodot (flourished 1695–1700); François Timoléon, abbé de Choisy (1644–1724); and François Fénelon (1651–1715). Of the male storytellers, only Perrault produced tales of lasting significance. In the 1690s the genre of the tale was considered a female prerogative, "women's province," "literally, like a feminine genre,"[3] according to the misogynistic Abbé de Villiers.[4] It is thus pertinent to take a closer look at the circle of women storytellers—or *conteuses*—who constituted a brilliant constellation of authors linked with one another through close networks of family and socioliterary friendships. We shall not deal here with notions of gender or of feminine writing, but with the striking literary landscape of the "second preciosity"[5] at the end of the seventeenth century.

The *conteuses* of the second preciosity, born roughly in the same generation,[6] came together initially through family ties. Murat and La Force were related to each other. La Force was related to the powerful Barjot family, to which d'Auneuil also belonged. Lhéritier was Perrault's niece,[7] and in the preface of her tale "Marmoisan"[8] she addressed Charles Perrault's son Pierre Darmancour and dedicated the tale to his "sister."[9]

Apart from family ties, friendships also united Lhéritier, d'Aulnoy, and Murat. Lhéritier, for instance, addressed one of her tales to the "beautiful countess" Murat, urging her to enter the ranks of the *conteuses*, as part of an amicable rivalry.[10] An obviously female cast of characters predominates in the tales' dedications: d'Auneuil dedicated her *Tiranie des fées détruite* (*The Tyranny of Fairies Destroyed*) to the duchess of Burgundy; Durand put her *Petits Soupers* (*Little Suppers*) under the protection of the duchess d'Orléans; the Princess de Conti was the dedicatee of Murat's *Contes des fées* (*Fairy Tales*); while d'Aulnoy dedicated several of her tale collections to the Princess Palatine, Charlotte-Elisabeth d'Orléans, who was Louis XIV's sister-in-law. The fact that a large proportion of the tales published by women was put under the protection of eminent women corroborates the then-prevailing concept of a feminine specificity of the fairy-tale genre. That female component was readily apparent in the dramatic expansion of the genre at the end of the seventeenth century and its continuation in the eighteenth century.

Equally remarkable is the exceptional relationship, largely unknown today, that developed between Lhéritier and two prominent *précieuses*, Antoinette Deshoulières and Madeleine de Scudéry. Brought together by emotional as well as intellectual and literary affinities, the three women developed a deep friendship and eventually formed an illustrious literary trio: Scudéry addressed her last verses to Lhéritier,[11] who herself dedicated to Scudéry the book she had just devoted to the memory of their mutual friend Deshoulières. When Deshoulières died in 1694, Lhéritier praised her as the tenth muse of Parnassus in her panegyric, *Le Parnasse reconnaissant ou Le Triomphe de Madame Des-Houlières, reçue dixième muse au Parnasse* (*Parnassus Grateful or The Triumph of Madame Des-Houlières*). *L'Apothéose de Mademoiselle de Scudéry* (*The Apotheosis of Mademoiselle de Scudéry*, 1702), another text by Lhéritier in the same vein, celebrated Madeleine de Scudéry as the "illustrious Sappho." Deshoulières herself vowed friendship to La Force, to whom she dedicated *Epître chagrine*[12] (*Sorrowful Epistle*).

The women's friendly relationships were not confined to dedications and praise; they also manifested themselves in the salons in which most of the *conteuses* participated as visitors or hostesses. In the biographical note of the 1785 edition of the *Cabinet des fées* (*The Chamber of the Fairies*), d'Auneuil's salon, mentioned briefly and long after the fact, was described as "open to all the wits and to all the women who wrote." As for the salon that Lhéritier hosted twice a week, literary tradition has made it the continuation of Scudéry's, which is confirmed in her obituary by *Le Journal des sçavans*, the earliest scholarly journal published in Europe: "Mademoiselle Lhéritier was linked to all the illustrious people of her century. [. . .] A society whose literature and friendship were also linked gathered [at her residence] [. . .] Several ladies even more distinguished by their wit than their rank came regularly to these assemblies."[13]

Those "ladies distinguished by their wit" were probably[14] Lhéritier's friends, Marie-Catherine d'Aulnoy and Henriette-Julie de Murat, as well as Catherine Bernard, who was known to have frequented her salon. In this way salons united most of the *conteuses* from the 1690s in a quasicoherent network of salon meetings that constituted a privileged setting for literary exchanges among brilliant and witty society women. Furthermore, storytelling, a salon pastime that had been popular among people of letters and women of high social standing since the 1650s, fostered tale composition and amicable competition among the *conteuses* and the *conteurs* (men storytellers) who were socially acquainted. Such games gave rise to several instances of different writers penning their own version of the same tale.[15]

Nearly all of the *conteuses* received public recognition for their talents, either socially or officially. *Le Mercure galant*, France's fashionable gazette and literary magazine, tirelessly praised the *conteuses*' delicacy, refinement, naturalness, and good taste. They were also praised for the jewel of fashionable culture, excellence in conversation, at which Marie-Catherine d'Aulnoy seemed particularly brilliant: "Her vivid and cheerful conversation was well above her books,"[16] according to Henriette-Julie de Murat. Admiration for Lhéritier's "conversation [which] had the charm of cheerfulness" appeared in the *Journal des Savants*.[17]

The *conteuses* accumulated a variety of literary awards. Lhéritier was honored by Caen's Académie des Palinots (Academy of the Palinots)[18] as early as 1692. Madame Durand was presented with an award by the French Academy (1701); Catherine Bernard was so honored three times (1691, 1693, and 1697). Toulouse's *Académie des Jeux Floraux* (Academy of Floral Games) heaped accolades on Catherine Bernard in 1696, 1697, and 1698, while Henriette-Julie de Murat was honored in Toulouse's Académie des Lanternistes (Academy of the Lanternists) three times (1695, 1696, and 1697).

Five of the seven *conteuses* were elected to Padua's Accademia degli Ricovrati[19] (Academy of the Inpatients), which named each of its "muses" evocatively: d'Aulnoy was the "eloquent," La Force was the "engaging," and Bernard was the "invincible." There, too, the first elected "muse" was Sappho, the "universal" (Scudéry), followed by Deshoulières, both good friends of Lhéritier. It was a world of high-achieving, seriously writing, and publicly acclaimed women, whose work complemented the taste of the times. Except for d'Aulnoy, they and their work were largely forgotten after their deaths until Mary Elizabeth Storer restored them to life in the 1920s. When her pioneering literary detective work, in itself necessarily incomplete and often incorrect, was resumed at the end of the twentieth and beginning of the twenty-first centuries, the lives, interrelationships, and bibliographies of the individual women writers were reconstituted for the first time in three centuries.

Notes

1. See Robert, 75–77, for a list of fairy tales that were published between 1690 and 1709 and 311–46 for the "phenomenon as a vogue."
2. Soriano, 1: 1025.
3. Timmermans, 218.
4. Villiers, 76. (Abbé de Villiers, *Entretiens sur les contes de fées* [Paris: J. Collombat, 1699].)

5. This is to paraphrase the title of Sophie Raynard's study on the phenomenon (see "Secondary Literature").

6. Of the seven *conteuses* that we mentioned, three were born around 1650, two others in 1662 and 1664, and the last in 1670.

7. See the biography of Marie-Jeanne Lhéritier de Villandon to see the precise family connection, in Lhéritier, p. 1, line 5.

8. "Marmoisan" was inserted by Lhéritier in her *Œuvres mêlées*. Paris: Guignard, 1696.

9. We have no record of the Perrault "sister." Consequently, we do not know to whom Lhéritier was referring. See the biography of Charles Perrault, in Perrault, p. 2, lines 24–30.

10. Lhéritier inserted this remark in her tale "L'Adroite Princesse ou les Aventures de Finette," first published in *Œuvres mêlées*.

11. *Le Journal des sçavans* January 1734 (833), "Éloge de Mademoiselle Lhéritier."

12. That *Epître* was reproduced by Vertron in *La Nouvelle Pandore* (Paris: Veuve Mazuel, 1698) 1: 330–39.

13. Regarding Scudéry's last verses, see *Le Journal des sçavans* January 1734, which contains the "Éloge de Mademoiselle Lhéritier" (833, 835, 836).

14. That d'Aulnoy, Bernard, and Murat may have been the distinguished ladies to whom Lhéritier referred here is speculation based on circumstantial biographical evidence. See the biographies of Lhéritier, d'Aulnoy, and Murat included in the present book.

15. Examples of tales in two versions include Perrault's "Les Fées" ("The Fairies") and Lhéritier's "Les Enchantements de l'Éloquence" ("The Enchantments of Eloquence"), Murat's "Le Roi Porc" ("The King Pig"), and d'Aulnoy's "Le Prince Marcassin" ("The Prince Boar"); Bernard's and Perrault's "Riquet à la houppe" ("Riquet with the Tuft"). Perrault's "Le Petit Poucet" ("Tom Thumb") and his "Cendrillon" ("Cinderella") appear consolidated in d'Aulnoy's "Finette Cendron."

16. Murat's words about her friend d'Aulnoy, quoted by Storer (24) from *Ouvrages de Madame la comtesse de Murat* [manuscript], Bibliothèque de l'Arsenal, MS #3471 (173).

17. *Le Journal des sçavans* January 1734 (836), "Éloge de Mademoiselle Lhéritier."

18. "Palinot" is a poem dedicated to the Immaculate Conception of the Virgin Mary.

19. In *La Nouvelle Pandore*, Vertron lists the "French Muses, or the illustrious ladies of France, qualified at the Accademia degli Ricovrati" (1:425–32). The five *conteuses* in question are d'Aulnoy, Lhéritier (both elected in 1697), Murat, La Force, and Bernard (all three elected unanimously in 1699). Scudéry and Deshoulières had preceded them in the early 1680s. It was customary for members to adopt mocking or self-denigrating titles for their academies.

Secondary Literature

Gheeraert, Tony, Perrault, Fénelon, Mailly, Préchac, Choisy et anonymes. *Contes merveilleux*. Paris: Honoré Champion, 2005.

Jasmin, Nadine. *Naissance du conte féminin: Madame d'Aulnoy*. Paris: Honoré Champion, 2002.

——. Madame d'Aulnoy. *Les Contes des Fées* suivis des *Contes nouveaux ou Les Fées à la Mode*. Ed. N. Jasmin. Paris: Honoré Champion, 2004. 2d ed. 2008: Champion Classiques.

Patard, Geneviève. Madame de Murat, *Contes*. Paris: Honoré Champion, 2006.

Raynard, Sophie. *La Seconde préciosité. Floraison des conteuses de 1690 à 1756*. Biblio 17, 130. Tübingen: Gunter Narr, 2002.

Robert, Raymonde. *Le Conte de fées littéraire en France de la fin du XVIIe à la fin du XVIIIe siècle en France*. Paris: Champion, [1982] 2002.

——, Mlle Lhéritier, Mademoiselle Bernard, Mademoiselle de La Force, Madame Durand, Madame d'Auneuil, *Contes*. Paris: Honoré Champion, 2005.

Storer, Mary Elizabeth. *Un Episode littéraire de la fin du XVIIe siècle. La Mode des contes de fées (1685–1700)*. [1928] Genève: Droz, 1972.

Timmermans, Linda. *L'Accès des femmes à la culture (1598–1715): Un débat d'idées de François de Sales à la marquise de Lambert*. Paris: Champion, 1993.

Charles Perrault

1628–1703

Yvette Saupé and Jean-Pierre Collinet
(translated and adapted by Sophie Raynard)

Charles Perrault was the son of a lawyer in the Parliament of Paris, Pierre Perrault († 1652), and of Paquette Leclerc († 1657). He and his twin brother, François, were born on 12 January 1628 in Paris and were baptized the day after their birth in the church of Saint-Etienne-du-Mont. François, however, lived for only six months. Charles had four surviving brothers. The eldest, Jean (1610–69), was a lawyer; Pierre (1611–79) was the chief treasurer of the City of Paris (1654–64); Claude (1613–88), to whom Charles was particularly close, was a doctor of medicine and later an architect and member of the Academy of the Sciences; and the youngest was Nicolas (1624–62), a doctor in theology who was expelled from the Sorbonne for having defended Antoine Arnauld and the Jansenists in 1655 and 1656. Charles Perrault came from a close-knit family with a bourgeois, Catholic, and cultured background, whose taste for novelty was combined with a vivid interest in letters, the sciences, and the arts.

Between 1636 and 1637, Charles entered secondary school at the Collège de Beauvais. Although he was a brilliant pupil, he was forced to drop out in his junior year, following an altercation with his tutor, around 1644. He and his friend Beaurain pursued their studies on their own for three or four more years, translating Latin authors and studying the Bible. On 27 July 1651, Charles passed his examination in law at the Université d'Orléans, but during his lifetime he pled only two cases. He then worked for his brother Pierre as a clerk and continued doing so from 1654 to 1663. Burlesque literature was then in vogue, and the two youngsters, aided by their brothers Nicolas and Claude, took part in it. They parodied the sixth song of the *Aeneid*, and in their excitement, they selected a minor episode from the *Iliad* as inspiration for a second travesty, the first book of *Les Murs de Troye*[1] (*The Walls of Troy*) published in 1653. In their burlesque satires, consistent with the critical spirit of the Perrault family, the young writers systematically deprecated the gods and the heroes of classic mythology in a manner that heralded Charles's later *Parallèle des Anciens et des Modernes* (*Parallel of the Ancients and the Moderns*). Charles continued to read as widely as he could. For instance, his brother Pierre had acquired the library of Germain Habert, a great wit of his time, and Charles found inspiration in its volumes for the *précieux* poems that were then in vogue.

Introduced by his brother Pierre to the superintendent Nicolas Foucquet, Charles met the greatest minds of his time at Vaux-le-Vicomte, Foucquet's palatial residence: Madeleine de Scudéry, Paul Pellisson, Pierre Corneille, Georges de Brébeuf, and Paul Scarron. Perrault frequented the witty *précieux* salons, for which occasions he composed verse in praise of hostesses and their guests. Following the *précieux* taste of the time, he composed *Le Portrait d'Iris* (*The Portrait of Iris*) and *Le Portrait de la Voix d'Iris* (*The Portrait of Iris' Voice*) in 1657 and 1658, which were printed in Jean Regnault de Segrais's collection of verbal portraits, *Recueil de Divers Portraits* (*Collection of Various Portraits*, 1659), as well as the *Dialogue de l'Amour et de l'Amitié* (*Dialogue on Love and Friendship*) in 1660, and finally the *Miroir ou la Métamorphose d'Orante* (*The Mirror or the Metamorphosis of Orante*) in 1661. The Pyrenees peace treaty signed in 1659, which ended the Franco-Spanish war,[2] inspired his *Ode sur la Paix* (*Ode on Peace*); he composed another ode in 1660 on the occasion of the marriage between Louis XIV and the infanta Marie-Thérèse of Spain, and a third one in 1661 on the occasion of the birth of their first son, the dauphin (heir to the throne).

Perrault's 1663 *Discours sur l'Acquisition de Dunkerque par le Roi* (*Discourse on the Acquisition of Dunkerque by the King*) brought him to the attention of Louis XIV's prime minister, Jean-Baptiste Colbert, who called Perrault into his service on 3 February 1663. With an annual compensation of fifteen hundred livres, raised to two thousand in 1669, Perrault was the secretary of the sessions of the "Little Academy." Founded by Colbert to create a public persona for Louis XIV as a brilliant king, the job of the Little Academy was to collect Latin legends for medals and mottoes for tapestries, monuments, and sculptures, as well as to review works dedicated to the glory of Louis XIV.

Family difficulties brought Perrault into dangerous waters with his employer, Colbert. His brother Pierre had been accused of mismanagement in his capacity of chief treasurer of the City of Paris, but when Perrault pled Pierre's case, Colbert remained inflexible. In consequence, Pierre had to sell the treasurership in 1664 at a great loss.[3] However, Charles's role with the minister subsequently grew up. Appointed first clerk of the royal buildings in 1665, he participated in planning the extension of the Louvre as well as the construction of Versailles. In a job that required conveying Colbert's orders to the projects' architects and dealing with trade associations, he brought in his brother Claude as architect. In 1667 a "Little Committee of the Louvre" (consisting of Louis Le Vau, principal architect of the king; Charles Le Brun, his principal painter; Claude; and Charles as his secretary) took on responsibility for renovating the façade of the Louvre. Giovanni Lorenzo Bernini, the leading Italian Baroque architect of his day, had refashioned Saint Peter's Basilica in Rome, and he was summoned from Rome with the expectation that he would lead the Louvre project. His plans, however, were discarded, and Claude's design for the colonnade of the Louvre was adopted, as Charles wrote in his *Mémoires (Memoirs)*.[4]

The Louvre expansion required Perrault to review architecture and decoration, examine estimates, manage payments, inspect completed work, and keep Colbert apprised of progress. At the same time, as Colbert's spokesperson and advisor, Perrault was responsible for attending sessions of the Academy of Painting and Sculpture. During this period Perrault's writings were inspired by his bureaucratic functions: his poem *La Peinture (On Painting)* in 1667, after a long series of mythological allusions, praised Le Brun in dithyrambs, as well as Louis XIV for having chosen him. He alluded to the gardens and the menagerie of Versailles, then under construction, and recalled the creation of the Royal Academy of Sciences, to which he had had his brother Claude admitted, and Claude's work on the construction of the Observatory of Paris. He invoked the paintings of Le Brun, some of which had served as patterns for Gobelin tapestries that illustrated major events of the early years of Louis XIV's reign. *La Peinture* solemnly celebrates the supremacy of his century's artists and the painters. In the same vein, and as the official glorifier of the monarch and his pomp, he composed *Le Parnasse poussé*

à bout (*Parnassus Pushed to the Extreme*) in 1668 as a letter to Jean Chapelain celebrating the recent occupation of Franche-Comté.[5]

Elected to the French Academy in 1671, Perrault introduced useful
reforms, such as elections with secret ballots, sessions with a fixed sched-
ule, use of a voting machine, and the creation of attendance tokens. Each
of the new practices ensured the regularity of the sessions and the timely
advancement of the Academy's major project, creating a dictionary of
the French language. From 1672 to 1674 Perrault served as chancellor of
the Academy, continuing to play an active role. In 1672, he also became
general controller of buildings, an office that Colbert created for him
with an annual stipend of three thousand livres. In these years Perrault's
career epitomized that of a successful court functionary.

Perrault's personal life changed in 1672, when, at the age of forty-
four, he married Marie Guichon. The nineteen-year-old daughter of a
low-ranking official (in charge of paying pensions contracted in Paris),
she brought a modest dowry of seventy thousand livres to the marriage.
They had three sons: Charles Samuel (25 May 1675–?), Charles (28
October 1676–?), and Pierre (21 March 1678–82 March 1700), all three
of whom were baptized in the church of Saint-Eustache.[6] The youngest,
Pierre, later took the surname Darmancour; it was he to whom his father
attributed his famous fairy tales.[7] After Charles's wife died of smallpox
in October 1678, he remained a widower and devoted himself to his
children's education.

In his public life in the 1670s, Charles bore two heavy responsibilities, his office as the controller of buildings and his role at the
French Academy. As a prominent intellectual he naturally participated
in literary disputes of his day. Thus in 1674 he espoused the cause of the
opera *Alceste* by Philippe Quinault and Giovanni Battista Lulli, when
he wrote *Critique de l'opéra ou Examen de la tragédie intitulée Alceste ou
le triomphe d'Alcide* (*Critique of the Opera or Examination of the Tragedy
Entitled Alcest or the Triumph of Alcid*). A public statement such as this
routinely elicited a response, and in this case Jean Racine responded the
following year in his preface to *Iphigénie* (1675), addressing the moderns'
criticisms of Euripides' *Alcest*. Racine, an ardent and confirmed Hellenist,
asserted that the moderns had misunderstood many passages in Euripides:
"I am certain that he is discounted by them solely because they have
misread the work on the basis of which they condemn him. I advise
these gentlemen not to decide so lightly about the works of the Ancients.
Such a man as Euripides at least deserved that they examine him since
they were so inclined to condemn him." Meant to put the moderns in

their place, this dismissive remark was one of the first attacks in the epic Quarrel of the Ancients and the Moderns. The moderns' irritation at the growing influence of Boileau and Racine—these two ancients later became the king's historiographers in 1677—may have been increased by their bias in favor of modern sensibilities and achievements. In 1675 J. B. Coignard published Perrault's *Recueil de divers ouvrages en prose et en vers* (*Collection of Various Works in Prose and Verse*), a collection of earlier writings, to which he had added *Le Labyrinthe de Versailles* (*The Labyrinth of Versailles*). In so doing, Charles rewrote a certain number of fables from La Fontaine's first collection (1668). The *Labyrinth*, which celebrated the charm of André Le Nôtre's grove in the park of Versailles, ornamented with fountain sculptures of Aesop's fables designed by Charles Le Brun. Perrault returned to the genre of the fable in his verse translation from Latin of *Les Fables de Faërne* (*Faerno's Fables*) in 1699, in which he was clearly competing with La Fontaine.

Charles ceased to collect his salary as the controller of buildings in 1680 and saw himself replaced by Colbert's own son, the marquis d'Ormoy, and excluded from the Little Academy. Although he signed his last official acts in 1683, he was nonetheless elected director of the French Academy.

From that point forward Perrault devoted himself to literary life and also continued to celebrate the major events of Louis XIV's reign. The 1682 birth of the Duke of Burgundy, Louis XIV's grandson, inspired *Le Banquet des dieux* (*The Banquet of the Gods*), in which he imagined himself accompanying Polymnia to a banquet of the gods on Mount Olympus, with each god singing in honor of the newborn prince, just as cheerful earthly companions would have done. With the burlesque tone of *The Walls of Troy* glimmering through the official tribute, Perrault's text was later put to music by Claude Oudot as an *opéra bouffe* and presented at the court before the child's mother, the dauphine.

The Marquise de Maintenon's influence precipitated a new climate of piety at court, consistent with which Perrault composed *Epître chrétienne sur la Pénitence* (*A Christian Epistle on Penitence*) in 1684, and immediately after the revocation of the Edict of Nantes (1685), Perrault penned an *Ode aux Nouveaux Convertis* (*Ode to the Newly Converted*). In 1686, he published *Saint-Paulin, évêque de Nole* (*Saint-Paulin, Bishop of Nole*), a poem in six stanzas dedicated to the renowned bishop and educator Jacques-Bénigne Bossuet.

On 27 January 1687, during a session at the French Academy, Charles Perrault's poem *Le Siècle de Louis le Grand* (*The Century of*

Louis the Great) was read aloud by the Abbé de Lavau. A tribute to Louis XIV, it claimed the superiority of the seventeenth century over the era of the Roman emperor Augustus and precipitated the Quarrel of the ancients and the moderns, arousing Nicolas Boileau-Despréaux's anger and Jean Racine's skepticism in the process. The quarrel marked a divide after which writers joined one of two camps: the ancients led by Nicolas Boileau-Despréaux, Jean Racine, Jean de La Fontaine, and Jean La Bruyère, or the moderns, whose leaders were Charles Perrault and Bernard le Bovier de Fontenelle. Perrault, with the four volumes of his *Parallel of the Ancients and the Moderns* (1688–97), played a vital role in the debate. Even though courtly flattery may have played a role when Perrault proclaimed the superiority of seventeenth-century authors over those of antiquity, the provocative positions he took represented sincerely held views. The quarrel that followed lasted ten years or so and was further embittered by personal rivalry and was punctuated by salvos aimed at each other by both party leaders.

Volume 3 of the *Parallel* is presented as a conversational stroll in the park of Versailles's palace with three characters, an Abbé (Perrault's eloquent spokesperson), a knight (more of a joker), and a president (defender of the ancients, as untalkative as he is unconvincing), on the topic of poetry. The *Parallel* tackles numerous themes, most of which return to criticisms of Homer's *Iliad* and *Odyssey* for lacking unity (because they consist of a succession of narratives that are independent from each other and lack verisimilitude). The *Parallel* prefers the Roman Virgil, in part because the moderns viewed him as conceptually more advanced, even though he had taken his inspiration from Homer, an argument that Boileau-Despréaux denounced as indefensible.

Boileau-Despréaux, not named but always present in *Parallel*, is accused of having dependence upon the Latin poet Horace. While the Abbé, a stand-in for Perrault, warmly praised Quinault's operas as well as Chapelain's *Pucelle* (*The Maid*) and defended the victims of Boileau-Despréaux's satires, he praised Corneille's tragedies but passed over those of Racine in silence. The moderns, according to *Parallel*, had created three new kinds of poetry: operas, gallant poetry, and the burlesque style.[8]

Perrault's detailed argumentation often leaves an impression of biased criticism, with selected passages, isolated from their context, as well as the highlighted details, occasionally sounding like deliberately satirical criticism with a burlesque tone.

To respond to the criticisms of the third volume of his *Parallel*, Perrault read (at a public session of the Academy in honor of François Fénelon's welcoming on 31 March 1693) a verse translation of the dialogue between Hector and Andromache from book 6 of *Iliad*, in order to demonstrate his admiration for Homer.

The exchange of ideas between the ancients and the moderns became an increasingly bitter personal quarrel, in particular between Boileau-Despréaux and Perrault, whose criticism of each other continued in their correspondence. In 1694, Boileau-Despréaux published *Réflexions critiques de Monsieur Despréaux sur Longin* (*Critical Reflections of Mr Despréaux on Longinus*), which set forth the test of time to judge masterpieces. Perrault composed *Apologie des femmes* (*Defense of Women*) in 1694 to counter Boileau-Despréaux's *Satire* X against women. Personal attacks cut to the quick, with Boileau-Despréaux accusing the Perrault family of "oddness." After the intercession of Antoine Arnauld, an exiled Jansenist, Boileau-Despréaux and Perrault publicly reconciled in the French Academy on 4 August 1694.

Perrault's championing of the moderns included the popular print of the *Bibliothèque bleue* (*The Blue Library*) of Troyes, and he tried his own hand at some of its popular topics. In 1691 Perrault's "La Marquise de Salusses ou la Patience de Grisélidis" ("Patient Griselda") was read aloud in the French Academy by the Abbé de Lavau. Known popularly as "Grisélidis" ("Griselda"), it was a short story derived from Boccaccio[9] via Petrarch and embellished with comments on seventeenth-century social and moral practices. In November 1693 Perrault produced a second popular tale, "Les Souhaits ridicules" ("The Ridiculous Wishes"), followed by "Peau d'âne" ("Donkeyskin") in 1694. When these three tales were published as elegantly versified *Contes en vers* (*Tales in* Verse), Charles added a preface in which he attacked the base humor of Milesian fables and insisted on the moral superiority of the tales he presented.

In 1697 Claude Barbin published *Histoires ou Contes du temps passé, avec des moralitez* (*Tales and Stories of the Past with Morals*), eight prose tales. Perrault's prose tales were inspired by a variety of sources,[10] such as the Italian literary tradition (Boccacio's *Decameron*,[11] Basile's *Pentameron*,[12] and Straparola's *Pleasant Nights*[13]) and the French literary tradition (*Les Chroniques de Perceforest*[13] or *The Chronicles of Perceforest*, Chrétien de Troyes' novels,[15] and Marie de France's lays[16]). Perrault's contribution, the elaboration of his narratives, led to a unique style. His narrative structure sometimes aimed at sobriety and dramatic briskness, as in "Le Petit Poucet" ("Tom Thumb"); sometimes achieved a rigorous symmetry, as in "Les Fées" ("The Fairies"); or climaxed in horrifying visions, as Blue Beard's wives "gaze at themselves in their clotted blood"[17] or the ogre's daughters lie abed with "their throats cut and swimming in their blood."[18]

In innumerable ways, Perrault made his *Tales* reflect seventeenth-century society: socially, they reflect the inventory of Blue Beard's furniture or the hierarchic listing in decreasing social order of slumbering Sleeping Beauty's court; stylistically, the prince's dithyrambic portrait in "Griselda" resembles those Perrault had written about Louis XIV; historically, the famine that forced Tom Thumb's family to lose their children recalls the sad reality of the terrible food shortages of 1693 and 1694, anchors this marvelous story socially, and heightens its credibility.

The tales also present a wide variety of genres: novellistic in "Cinderella," pastoral in "Griselda," and fabliaulike in "The Ridiculous Wishes." Similarly "The Little Red Riding Hood" is colored by sexual innuendo.

Perrault's irony distanced him from his narratives, allowing him to criticize characters in "Griselda" or to compose five different moralities in "Donkey Skin." His irony takes a mischievous turn when it stigmatizes women's coquetry ("Donkey Skin") or gently pokes fun at their impatience to get married (the moralities of "Sleeping Beauty"). Perrault's burlesque exaggeration highlights the deformities of the eponymous hero of "Riquet with the Tuft," whose depiction he seems to enjoy. Each narrative's unequaled density and depth contributed to Perrault's popularity as a storyteller.

Around the same time, Charles composed *Les Hommes illustres qui ont paru en France pendant le siècle avec leurs portraits au naturel* (*The Illustrious Men who appeared in France during the Century with their Natural Portraits*). A collection of one hundred portraits of illustrious men (2 vols., 1696 and 1700) begun by Michel Bégon, the "Intendant of La Rochelle, its illustrious men comprise . . .": twenty-two church men, fifteen ship captains, twenty statesmen and magistrates, twenty-nine scientists and men of letters, and fourteen craftsmen and painters. Some major figures, however, were excluded: Foucquet (in disgrace), La Rochefoucauld (previously involved in the Fronde, a widespread insurrection against Louis XIV's centralizing efforts), La Bruyère (a notorious ancient), and Scarron (the marquise de Maintenon's first husband). Louis XIV had enjoined Perrault to omit portraits of Antoine Arnauld and Blaise Pascal, prominent Jansenists. Prudently replaced in the first edition, Arnauld and Pascal were later reinserted. Perrault's duty as controller of the royal buildings had put him in direct contact with leading social figures and artists, and he completed the book's documentation by reading contemporary books.

Perrault's historical exactitude did not prevent him from praising his subjects extravagantly or from ignoring details that would detract from his heroes' glory. Thus, Perrault minimized the participation of Condé[19] in the Fronde. Perrault's friendships and enmities are everywhere apparent. For instance, he denigrated La Fontaine's *Fables* as simple translations or paraphrases of Aesop's *Fables* and overtly disapproved of the licentious aspect of La Fontaine's *Contes* (*Tales*). His tribute to Corneille was filled with enthusiasm, but Racine received far less attention. He celebrated the talent of Molière, comedian and author, and deliberately minimized literary criticism of his comedy *Tartuffe*.[20] His profoundly admiring tribute to Pascal resembles a panegyric. He vividly praised his brother Claude's talents as an architect and as a translator of Vitruvius's Latin tract on architecture as well as his scientific research. Well received, *The Illustrious Men* illustrated the thesis of the *Parallel* in claiming the superiority of seventeenth-century authors over those of antiquity, while perpetuating the antique tradition of Plutarch's *Lives* and those of Cornelius Nepos.

Perrault's last years were darkened by a somber affair. On 6 April 1697, his youngest son, Pierre, mortally injured a young neighbor, Guillaume Caulle, in a duel. Charles paid two thousand livres in damages, but his assets were nonetheless temporarily seized. On 2 March 1700, Pierre, then a lieutenant in the dauphin's regiment, died.

One of Perrault's last works, *Les Pensées chrétiennes* (*Christian Thoughts*, written 1694–c. 1702[21]) comprises thoughts revolving around a Christian believer's meditations, literary esthetics, and practical ethics.[22] Perrault, a firm believer, uses the Vulgate translation of the Bible and reflects on the world to come and on eternal happiness. The range of his meditations is broad in the extreme—Protestants' excessive intellectual curiosity; Catholic orthodoxy; essential differences between humans and animals; moral practices of his time, such as vanity and gambling; as well as general considerations—a journal of sorts that reflects his fundamental rationalism.

In the last years of his life Perrault also wrote *Mémoires de ma vie* (*Memoirs of My Life*), which remained unfinished and was published long after his death in 1759. He died during the night between the 15 and 16 May 1703 and was buried on 17 May in the nave of his parish church, Saint-Benoît.

Charles Perrault was a man of conscience who fulfilled his duties with seriousness and was concerned with efficacy. A zealous academician, he introduced reforms at the French Academy, which elected him as their chancellor and then their director for 1681. A zealous politician as well, Perrault became Colbert's closest advisor. He meant to be a man of his time, in tune with current events. As a public poet, he celebrated contemporary royal events, as was common practice at the time. Still, the broad variety of the literary genres he practiced demonstrates his broad interests. As an author of fables and tales, he competed with La Fontaine—or perhaps it was sheer admiration slightly tinged with jealousy. Nonetheless, he was a perfect *"honnête homme."*[23]

Notes

1. Les Frères Perrault et Beaurain, *Les Murs de Troye ou l'origine du burlesque*, book 1.

2. The Franco-Spanish War began with French entry in 1635 into the Thirty Years' War (1618–48), in which Spain was already a participant. Warfare between the two kingdoms continued until 1659, when the Treaty of the Pyrenees was signed.

3. Purchasing government offices was standard practice in seventeenth-century France.

4. This fact cannot be proven because Claude's blueprints and drawings burned in the fire of the Louvre's library in 1871. See Charles Perrault, *Les Mémoires de ma vie*, with a preface by Antoine Picon: "Un modèle paradoxal," *Art et Histoire*, Macula, 3rd trimester, 1993. Nonetheless, some claim that Le Vau was responsible for the Louvre design.

5. This is a reference to the War of Devolution, 1667–68. Philip IV of Spain died in 1665, and in 1667 Louis XIV claimed, in the name of his Spanish-born wife. Marie-Thérèse, some Spanish territories, a claim that Spain denied. France declared war, and French forces under the command of Turenne occupied Flanders while another French force under Condé took Franche-Comté (1668). Eventually Franche-Comté was returned to Spain under the Treaty of Aix-la-Chapelle, signed on 2 May 1668 which declared the end of the War of Devolution between France and Spain.

6. Marie-Jeanne Lhéritier de Villandon, Perrault's niece, is the only one who mentions the existence of a daughter, in the dedicatory letter to her tale "Marmoisan" (in *Oeuvres meslées*). Marc Soriano argues that she could have been Charles Perrault's firstborn: either in January or February 1673 or in June 1674 (*Les Contes de Perrault*, 318–20).

7. Charles Perrault published his *Tales* under the name of his youngest son, Pierre (Perrault) Darmancour (Armancour being the name of a property he had bought for him), probably fearful of criticism from the "ancients," according to F. Collin, *Charles Perrault, le fantôme du XVIIe siècle* (Draveil: Colline, 1999).

8. Burlesque is clearly defined, with Paul Scarron cited as a model and the burlesque of Boileau-Despréaux's *Lutrin* (*Lectern*) being less appreciated.

9. It is indeed Day X of Boccaccio's *Decameron*. Petrarch translated that novella into Latin in 1374 in a letter addressed to Boccaccio, "De obœdentia

et fide uxorial [. . .]" ("On the Obedience and Faithfulness of Wives [. . .]"), in which form the novella became a classic of chapbook literature.

10. Such as chapbook literature and *The Blue Library*.

11. A collection of 100 novellas, probably begun in 1350 and finished in 1353.

12. Neapolitan for *The Tale of Tales*, published posthumously in five fascicles by his sister Adriana in Naples, Italy, from 1634 to 1636.

13. Modeled on Boccacio's *Decamerone*.

14. A 1528 collection of French tales.

15. A French poet who flourished in the twelfth century.

16. A French woman poet of the late twelfth century.

17. Perrault, *Contes*, ed. Jean-Pierre Collinet, 151.

18. Ibid., 198.

19. Louis II de Bourbon, Prince de Condé (8 September 1621–11 November 1686), was a French general and the most famous representative of the Condé branch of the House of Bourbon.

20. The first *Tartuffe* was presented in 1664 at Versailles. The eponymous character, a hypocritically devout cleric, scandalized its audience, especially powerful men in the secretive "cabal of the devout" who were offended by the play. The archbishop of Paris and the first president of parliament were aggressively opposed to the production. As a result, a full production of the play was prohibited by the king. Eventually *Tartuffe* was presented again on 5 February 1669.

21. In the thought 75, Perrault mentions the death of the Jesuit Commire, on Christmas day 1702.

22. Some were published by Paul Bonnefon in 1901.

23. A seventeenth-century ideal of honorability and culture.

Charles Perrault's Works

Biographies

Les Hommes illustres qui ont paru en France pendant ce siècle avec leurs portraits au naturel (with the contribution of M. Bégon). Paris: A. Dezollier, 1696–1700.

Les Mémoires de ma vie [1699] unfinished autobiography, posthumous publication in 1759. Paris: Macula, 1993. (Available in English: *Charles Perrault: Memoirs of my Life*. Ed. and trans. Jeanne Morgan Zarucchi. Columbia: University of Missouri Press, 1989.)

Fables

Le Labyrinthe de Versailles [1675]. Paris: Edition de Moniteur, 1981.
Traduction des Fables *de Faërne*. Paris: Coignard, 1699.

Literary Criticism

Perrault, Charles et Claude, et Beaurain. *Les Murs de Troye, ou l'Origine du burlesque*. Paris: Louis Chamhoudry, 1653; *Livre I*. Ed. Yvette Saupé (*Biblio 17* 127) Tübingen: Gunter Narr, 2001.

Parallèle des Anciens et des Modernes. Paris: Coignard, 1688–97. Genève: Slatkine, 1971.

1688 – Volume 1: on the sciences and the arts.

1690 – Volume 2: on eloquence.

1692 – Volume 3: on poetry.

1697 – Volume 4: on astronomy, geography, navigation, war, philosophy, music, medicine, etc.

Devotional Writings

Pensées chrétiennes de Charles Perrault, ed. Jacques Barchilon and Catherine Velay-Vallantin. Paris-Seattle: Papers on French Seventeenth-Century Literature, 1987.

Tales (Signed Pierre Perrault Darmancour)

Histoires ou Contes du temps passé, avec des moralités. Paris: Barbin, 1697.

Secondary Literature

Barchilon, Jacques. *Perrault's Tales of Mother Goose*. 2 vols. New York: Pierpont Morgan Library, 1956. Bonnefon, Paul. "Charles Perrault, *essai sur sa vie et ses ouvrages*." *Revue d'Histoire littéraire de la France R.H.L.F.* 11 (1904): 365–420.

———. "Charles Perrault, *littérateur et académicien*." *Revue d'Histoire Littéraire de La France* 12 (1905): 549–610.

———. "*Les dernières années de Charles Perrault*." *Revue d'Histoire Littéraire de La France* 13 (1906): 606–75.

Collinet, Jean-Pierre. *Perrault. Contes, suivis du Miroir ou La Métamorphose d'Orante, De la Peinture, poème et du Labyrinthe de Versailles*. Paris: Gallimard, Folio, 1981.

Delarue, Paul. *Le Conte populaire français. Catalogue raisonné des versions de France et des pays de langue française*; vol. 1. Paris: Erasme, 1957, with the contribution of Marie-Louise Ténèze; vol. 2. Paris: Maisonneuve et Larose, 1965. (See Ténèze for vol. 3.)

Hannon, Patricia. *Fabulous Identities: Women's Fairy Tales in Seventeenth-Century France*. Amsterdam: Rodopi, 1998.

Lewis, Philip E. *Seeing through the Mother Goose Tales: Visual Turns in the Writings of Charles Perrault*. Stanford: Stanford University Press, 1996.

Robert, Raymonde. *Le Conte de fées littéraire en France de la fin du 17ème siècle à la fin du 18ème siècle*. Nancy: Presses universitaires de Nancy, 1982.

Saupé, Yvette. *Les Contes de Perrault et la mythologie. Rapprochements et influences*. Biblio 17, 104. Tübingen: Narr, 1997.

———. *Les Murs de Troye ou l'origine du burlesque*. Livre I. Biblio 17, 127. Tübingen: Narr, 2001.

Seifert, Lewis. *Fairy Tales, Sexuality, and Gender in France, 1690–1715: Nostalgic Utopias*. Cambridge Studies in French 55. Cambridge: Cambridge University Press, 1996.

Soriano, Marc. *Les Contes de Perrault, culture savante et traditions populaires*. Paris: Gallimard (N.R.F.), 1968.

———. *Le Dossier Perrault*. Paris: Hachette Littérature, 1972.

Storer, Mary Elizabeth. *Un Episode de la fin du XVIIème siècle. La mode des contes de fées* (1685–1700) [1928]. Paris: Champion, 1972.

Ténèze, Marie-Louise. *Le Conte populaire français. Catalogue raisonné des versions de France et des pays de langue française;* vol. 3. Paris: Maisonneuve et Larose, 1977. (See Delarue for vols. 1 and 2.)

Velay-Vallantin, Catherine. *L'Histoire des contes*. Paris: Fayard, 1992.

Marie-Catherine Le Jumel de Barneville, Baroness d'Aulnoy

1650/51?–1705

Nadine Jasmin
(translated and adapted by Sophie Raynard)

Very little concrete information exists about Marie-Catherine, born Le Jumel de Barneville, and consequently hypotheses join the few existing facts[1] about the full and novelistic life she is said to have led. She was born in 1650 or 1651 into a solidly aristocratic Norman family. Her father died when she was very young, and her mother, Judith-Angélique de Saint-Pater, married the Marquis de Gudanes, who later disappeared from her life, whether by separation or by death is unknown.

In 1666 the young Marie-Catherine was married to a man thirty years her senior, François de la Motte, Baron d'Aulnoy. A friend of her mother and of her mother's lover, the Marquis de Courboyer, the Baron encountered financial difficulties when his patron the Duke de Vendôme died, leaving him without a regular income. Baron d'Aulnoy then tried his hand at finance, but his operations, not altogether orderly, incurred legal penalties, and his earlier business with Nicolas Fouquet, now in disgrace, led to further prosecution by Louis XIV's prime minister, Jean-

---

*Marie-Catherine is often referred to as Countess d'Aulnoy, but since she married a baron, "baroness" is a more accurate title than "countess."

Baptiste Colbert. The baron's financial difficulties inevitably worsened marital problems, with the result that Marie-Catherine withdrew for long periods of time to her mother's Paris residence in the Rue de l'Université.

During the first years of her marriage, the young Madame d'Aulnoy had given birth at eleven-month intervals to three children, all of whom were baptized at the Church of St. Gervais: Marie-Angélique (baptized on 26 January 1667 and apparently dead soon after), Dominique-César (baptized on 23 November 1667, also probably dead at a young age, as there is no later mention of him), and Marie-Anne (baptized on 30 October 1668, the first to survive).[2] Thirteen months later Marie-Catherine bore Judith-Henriette, baptized in the church of Saint-Sulpice on 14 November 1669. She also survived and later joined her grandmother, the Marquise de Gudanes, in Spain, where she married the Marquis de Bargente.

During her fourth pregnancy, d'Aulnoy's affairs took a dramatic turn. Her husband's miserable finances and his probable ill treatment of his wife impelled her to take shelter with her mother. The Marquise de Gudanes, in turn, plotted with her lover, the Marquis de Courboyer, together with two accomplices, to have Baron d'Aulnoy accused of lese-majesty.[3] However, the plot misfired and inculpated its perpetrators, who were imprisoned and found guilty.[4] Madame de Gudanes's lover was executed, and she herself went into exile in Spain, where she lived until her death in Madrid in 1702 and where she reputedly served as a spy in the service of the Spanish Habsburg and the French Bourbon monarchies.

When Madame de Gudanes fled France, Marie-Catherine was nearing the end of her pregnancy and could not travel with her. After giving birth to Judith-Henriette in November 1669 and still under order of arrest, she is said to have been imprisoned in the Conciergerie in Paris (in December 1669). Because of her mother's highly placed connections, or perhaps even because of her husband's intervention (since he had never formally accused her of complicity in his mother-in-law's plot), she seems to have been soon released, at which point she is said to have spent at least a year in a convent. By 1672 she was again free.[5]

D'Aulnoy may have traveled to Flanders (1672–73) and England (1675), probably returned to Paris around 1676–1677, and may have joined her mother in Spain in 1679. She is said to have traveled again to England in 1682,[6] before returning permanently to France in 1685. Scattered information, which may or may not be reliable, exists for her travels,[7] but hard evidence is notably absent.

During the years between 1672 and 1690, Marie-Catherine d'Aulnoy, estranged from her husband, gave birth to two daughters of unknown paternity: Thérèse-Aimée was baptized in Saint-Sulpice on 14 October 1676 (which demonstrates Madame d'Aulnoy's residence in Paris at that time); Françoise-Angélique, for whom no baptism certificate has been found, is commonly said to have been born in 1677, but the *Mercure galant* reported her death in December 1677 "at about five years"[8] of age, which effectively dates her birth considerably earlier. Thérèse-Aimée, who was known as Madame de Préaux d'Antigny in adulthood, resided in Spain and never married. It is possible, even probable, that she accompanied her mother to Spain in 1679 or 1680, a journey that later inspired Madame d'Aulnoy's *Mémoires de la cour d'Espagne* (*Memoirs of the Court of Spain*, 1690) and *Relation du voyage d'Espagne* (*Travels into Spain, Being the Ingenious and Diverting Letters of the Lady *** Travels into Spain*, 1691).

By 1690, Madame d'Aulnoy was again in Paris, where she had circulated two religious tracts (*Sentiments d'une Ame pénitente* and *Le Retour d'une Ame à Dieu*), in manuscript forms. Given royal permission to be published in 1691 and 1692 (although not printed until 1698), these devotional writings must have smoothed her reentry into fashionable Paris literary life (in the 1690s repentance was in vogue both at Louis XIV's court and in society), where questions about events in the previous twenty years seem to have been ignored. Until her death, her salon was among the city's most popular, frequented by princes and leading aristocrats.[9]

In 1690 Marie-Catherine also attended the salon of Anne-Thérèse de Marguenat de Courcelles, Marquise de Lambert (which had opened in 1682), where she came into contact with François Timoléon, abbé de Choisy, François Fénelon, and fellow *conteuses* Catherine Bernard, Charlotte-Rose de La Force, and Henriette-Julie de Murat. At the same time, according to her fellow *conteuse* Murat, d'Aulnoy was also conducting her own salon in the Rue Saint-Benoît.[10] According to Anne-Marguerite du Noyer, her salon was attended by English aristocrats of the Protestant diaspora. In both these salons her tales were probably read aloud long before their publication in 1697.

D'Aulnoy published her first novel, *Histoire d'Hypolite, comte de Duglas* (*Hypolitus, Earl of Douglas*, 1690), which established her reputation as a successful author. The favorable reception of the embedded tale entitled "L'Ile de la félicité" ("The Island of Happiness") in that novel prompted her to compose and publish collections of further such tales in 1697 and 1698. The 1690s, crucial years for d'Aulnoy, defined her literary career and brought her recognition both in France and in England.

Marie-Catherine died on 12 or 13 January 1705 at her house in rue Saint-Benoît, her funeral celebrated in Saint-Sulpice on 14 January 1705.[11] She left behind a solid reputation as a woman of letters and was survived by four daughters, although no further descendants can be traced.

Like Perrault, d'Aulnoy seemed to regard her tales as a minor part of her overall literary production and was more acclaimed for her gallant novels and her historical memoirs. As a skillful polygraph, she had tried various genres: two works of piety, four volumes of historical memoirs, three novels, and one collection of gallant short stories, in addition to the eight volumes of tales published in 1697 and 1698 for which she is now best known. The entirety of her literary production was published at a sustained rate of one to two titles per year, principally between 1690 and 1698. With an obvious literary and business flair,[12] d'Aulnoy exploited the fashionability of literary vogues among highly placed book buyers of her day: the novella, which, since the middle of the century, had replaced the long heroic novel; the gallant short story; the historical memoir; and the short story.[13]

When d'Aulnoy published her eight volumes of fairy tales in 1697 and 1698, she was already well known by a public that, ever since the publication of *Hypolitus*, had eagerly anticipated further works. D'Aulnoy's insertion of a marvelous tale into that sentimental and gallant novel probably contributed to its success. At the very least, *Hypolitus* marks the official birth, in the literary history of the genre, of the French literary fairy tale. The years 1697 and 1698, in particular, were years of abundance for the marvelous, with more than sixty tales published.

The first four of Madame d'Aulnoy's eight volumes of tales appeared as *Contes des fées* (*Tales of the Fairies*) in 1697. The second four volumes, entitled *Contes nouveaux ou les Fées à la mode* (*New Tales, or Fairies in Fashion*) appeared in 1698. A clever woman of letters, d'Aulnoy thus enjoyed a dual success: in literary terms, she had chosen a genre then at its peak, and in personal terms she had skillfully managed her literary career.

Famous for all of her works three centuries ago, d'Aulnoy's fame diminished rapidly after her death, and she survives in today's collective memory as the author of her *contes de fées*. However, d'Aulnoy's ultimate success remains ambiguous, for individual tales from her oeuvre have long been submerged by a flood of incorrect attributions, her collections have appeared in truncated form, and they have been adapted for varying social and age readerships in translation in the course of which d'Aulnoy came close to losing her identity and her tales their soul, their richness, and their charm, as their astonishing vitality was often excised from the entirety of her original tales.

Notes

1. For a detailed biographical update, see Jacques Barchilon's study in the introduction of the following edition on d'Aulnoy: *Madame d'Aulnoy, Contes I*, ed. Philippe Hourcade (Paris: S.T.F.M., 1997): v–xxv. Barchilon refers to the works of R. Foulché-Delbosc, M. E. Storer, J. Roche-Mazon, and O. Ranum (for the last three, see secondary literature).

2. Marie-Anne later married and became Madame de Hèere.

3. In civil law, *lese-majesty* refers to any offence against the sovereign authority. It often counted as high treason.

4. Documentation about the plot is to be found in Roche-Mazon and Ranum's pieces (see secondary literature). Both critics took the information from archival sources (see biographical sources).

5. According to Roche-Mazon, 122.

6. Where she met and became friends with her compatriot Saint-Evremond.

7. There are no historical documents available, but d'Aulnoy herself—especially in the prefaces of her "historical" novels—mentions that she traveled to those countries. For instance, in the dedication of her first novel, she evoked "the foreign courts" she claimed to have frequented. It could very well have just been an artifice since it was common practice to pretend to have traveled abroad when writing such pieces. However, regarding the trip to Spain in particular, Roche-Mazon's study entitled "Le voyage d'Espagne de Madame d'Aulnoy" is quite convincing.

8. See Roche-Mazon, "Le voyage d'Espagne de Mme d'Aulnoy."

9. See Dorothy Disse, "Marie-Catherine d'Aulnoy" (online in *Other Women's Voices*).

10. Her salon is mentioned by contemporaries such as Henriette-Julie de Murat in her handwritten journal: *Ouvrages de Madame la comtesse de Murat* [manuscript], in MS 3471 (173–74), cited by Storer (24): "mille gens venaient chez elle" ("hundred of people came to her place").

11. Per the funeral notice included in her archives at the Bibliothèque Nationale.

12. Her editorial flair is attested to by her choosing to have almost all of her works published by Barbin, the fashionable publisher of her time, who

specialized in mondain literature. Among her novels and memoirs, only *Histoire d'Hypolite* (published by L. Sevestre) and *Le Comte de Warwick* (Compagnie des Libraires Associés) were not published by Barbin.

13. In regard to the diversification of the novel, read M. Lever, *Romanciers du Grand Siècle*, "L'âge classique" (173–264), and, in particular, "L'âge d'or du 'petit roman'" (206–26) (Paris: Fayard, 1996).

Marie-Catherine d'Aulnoy's Works

Fairy Tales

"L'Île de la Félicité." *Histoire d'Hypolite, comte de Duglas*, "Seconde partie," 143–81. Paris: Sevestre, 1690.

Les Contes des Fées. Par Madame D**. 4 vols. Paris: Claude Barbin, 1697. [Vols. 3 and 4 are nowhere to be found in French public libraries, and according to Jacques Barchilon, it is most probably the case for major European libraries.]

Contes Nouveaux ou Les Fées à la mode. Par Madame D**. Vols. 1 and 2. Paris: Veuve de Théodore Girard, 1698.

Suite des Contes Nouveaux ou des Fées à la mode. Par Madame D**. Vols. 3 and 4. Paris: Nicolas Gosselin, 1698.

Madame d'Aulnoy. *Les Contes des Fées* suivis des *Contes nouveaux ou Les Fées à la Mode*, ed. N. Jasmin. Paris: Honoré Champion, 2004 (second edition 2008: Champion Classiques).

Historical Novels and Memoirs

Histoire d'Hypolite, comte de Duglas. 2 vols. Paris: Louis Sevestre, 1690; ed. with an introduction by Shirley Jones Day. London: Institute of Romance Studies, 1994.

Mémoires de la Cour d'Espagne. 2 vols. Paris: Claude Barbin, 1690.

Relation du voyage d'Espagne. 3 vols. Paris: Claude Barbin, 1691; ed. R. Fouché-Delbosc. Paris: Klincksieck, 1926; ed. M. Susana Seguin. Paris: Desjonquères, 2005.

Histoire de Jean de Bourbon, Prince de Carency. 3 vols. Paris: Claude Barbin, 1692.

Nouvelles espagnoles. Par Madame D***. 2 vols. Paris: Claude Barbin, 1692.

Nouvelles ou Mémoires historiques, Contenant ce qui s'est passé de plus remarquable dans l'Europe [. . .], Par Madame D***. 2 vols. Paris: Claude Barbin, 1693.

Mémoires de la Cour d'Angleterre. Par Madame D***. 2 vols. Paris: Claude Barbin, 1695.

Le Comte de Warwick. Par Madame d'Aulnoy. 2 vols. Paris: Compagnie des Libraires Associez, 1703.

Secondary Literature

Historical Sources

Archives de la Bastille. Vol. 7: vi, 335–41. Paris: F. Ravaisson, 1874 [on the plot and the trial].

Cabinet de d'Hosier 250, Factum pour François de la Motte. Paris: Bibliothèque Nationale de France [on the plot and the trial].

Cabinet de d'Hosier 250, no. 6633, Factum rédigé par le baron d'Aulnoy [on the plot and the trial].

Files from the parishes Saint-Gervais and Saint-Sulpice, in Ms. Fr. no. 32593. Paris: Bibliothèque Nationale [on Madame d'Aulnoy's children].

Critical Sources

Biancardi, Elisa. "À propos de Madame d'Aulnoy: Esthétique galante et genèse des contes de fées." *Il Confronto letterario* 37.1 (2002): 73–90.

———. "De Madeleine de Scudéry à Madame d'Aulnoy. Esthétique galante et merveilleux." In *Madeleine de Scudéry, une femme de lettres au XVIIᵉ siècle,* ed. D. Denis et A-E. Spica. Arras: Artois Presses Université, 2003, 231–40.

Defrance, Anne. *Les Contes de fées et les nouvelles de Madame d'Aulnoy (1690– 1698). L'imaginaire féminin à rebours de la tradition.* Genève: Droz, 1998.

Duggan, Anne E. *Salonnières, Furies, and Fairies: The Politics of Gender and Cultural Change in Absolutist France.* Newark: University of Delaware Press, 2005.

Hannon, Patricia. *Fabulous Identities: Women's Fairy Tales in Seventeenth-Century France.* Amsterdam, Atlanta: Rodopi, 1998.

Harries, Elizabeth Wanning. *Twice upon a Time: Women Writers and the History of the Fairy Tale.* Princeton: Princeton University Press, 2001.

Jasmin, Nadine. *Naissance du conte féminin. Mots et merveilles: Les contes de fées de Madame d'Aulnoy (1690–1698).* Paris: Champion, 2002.

Jones, Christine. "The Poetics of Enchantment (1690–1715)." *Marvels and Tales* 17.1 (2003): 55–74.

Mainil, Jean. *Madame d'Aulnoy et le rire des fées: Essai sur la subversion féerique et le merveilleux comique sous l'Ancien Régime.* Paris: Kimé, 2001.

Ranum, Orest. "Contestation et devoir civique: Le piège monté contre le sieur de la Motte d'Aulnoy." In *Ordre et contestation au temps des classiques* (Biblio 17, 73), 2: 233–39. Tübingen: Narr, 1992.

Roche-Mazon, Jeanne. "Madame d'Aulnoy et son mari" and "Le Voyage d'Espagne de Mme d'Aulnoy." In *Autour des contes de fées.* Paris: Didier, 1968. 7–20, 95–150.

Seifert, Lewis C. "Marie-Catherine le Jumel de Barneville, Comtesse d'Aulnoy." In *French Women Writers: A Bio-Bibliographical Source Book,* ed. E. M. Sartori and D. W. Zimmerman. New York: Greenwood, 1991. 11–20.

――――. *Fairy Tales, Sexuality, and Gender in France, 1690–1715: Nostalgic Utopias* (Cambridge Studies in French 55). Cambridge: Cambridge University Press, 1996.

Sermain, Jean-Paul. *Métafictions (1670–1730). La réflexivité dans la littérature d'imagination.* Paris: Champion, 2002.

――――. Le Conte de fées, du Classicisme aux Lumières. Paris: Desjoncquères, 2005.

Sterckx, Christiane. "Le Passage au stade adulte dans cinq contes de fées de Madame d'Aulnoy." In *Recherches sur le conte merveilleux*, ed. G. Jacques. Louvain-la-Neuve: Travaux de la Faculté de Philosophie et Lettres de l'Université Catholique de Louvain, 1981. 73–100.

Storer, Mary Elizabeth. "Madame d'Aulnoy." In *Un Épisode littéraire de la fin du XVIIème siècle: La Mode des contes de fées (1685–1700)* [1928]. Geneva: Droz, 1972.

Welch, Marcelle Maistre. "Les Jeux de l'écriture dans les contes de fées de madame d'Aulnoy." *Romanische Forschungen*, 101.1 (1989): 75–80.

――――. "La Satire du rococo dans les contes de fées de Madame d'Aulnoy." *Revue Romane*, 28.1 (1993): 75–85.

Zimmermans, Margarete. "'Il le croqua comme un poulet': Discours alimentaire chez Madame d'Aulnoy." *Biblio* 17, 86 (1994): 537–55.

Zuerner, Adrienne E. "Reflections of the Monarchy in d'Aulnoy's Belle-Belle ou le Chevalier Fortuné." In *Out of the Woods: The Origins of the Literary Fairy Tale in Italy and France*, ed. Nancy Canepa. Detroit: Wayne State University Press, 1997. 194–217.

Catherine Bernard

1663?–1712

Lewis C. Seifert

Catherine Bernard was born in Rouen, probably on 24 August 1663, in all likelihood to a wealthy merchant family.[1] In spite of several biographers' claims, it is doubtful that she was related to the illustrious Corneille brothers, Pierre and Thomas. Rouen's lively intellectual atmosphere is bound to have encouraged Bernard's literary interests, but nothing is known of her early education or contacts there. At some point she made her way to Paris and became well known for her "gallant" works, as they were called by *Le Mercure galant*, the premier literary review of seventeenth-century France. The same *Mercure galant* announced her abjuration of Protestantism and her conversion to Catholicism after the revocation of the Edict of Nantes in 1685.

Never married, Bernard was known to many of the literary and social elite of her day. Among her most important acquaintances was the writer and philosopher Bernard Le Bovier de Fontenelle (1657–1757), to whom several modern critics have attributed Bernard's works and with whom she may have been romantically involved. In any case, seventeenth-century observers viewed their relationship as one of friendly collaboration, a relationship that evokes a type of authorship common in seventeenth-century salon circles.[2] Bernard's involvement in these circles was undoubtedly decisive for her literary ambitions, but we possess little specific information about the nature or the extent of her activities.

Still, there is substantial evidence that she was active in the literary scene of her day. Between 1680 and 1696, she published five novels, staged and published two plays, and wrote another play that was read but not staged. She was also well known as a poet, with many pieces anthologized both during her lifetime and after her death. Bernard's literary reputation was equally substantial. She won prizes in poetry competitions sponsored by the French Academy in 1691, 1693, and 1697, and by Toulouse's Académie des Jeux Floraux (the Academy of Floral Games) in 1696, 1697, and 1698; the Abbé Vertron lavished praise on her in his collection of portraits of "illustrious women" of the seventeenth century;[3] in 1699 she earned honorary membership in Padua's Accademia degli Ricovrati (The Academy of the Sheltered); and in the last years of her life, even after she had ceased publishing her works, she continued writing poetry for highly placed nobles.[4]

In the midst of celebrity, Bernard was nonetheless bereft of financial security. In the early 1690s the devout Chancelière de Pontchartrain accorded her a meager pension, support that marked a dramatic shift in Bernard's interests. She stopped writing for the theater, participating in poetry contests, and, after her 1696 novel *Inès de Cordoue* with its two embedded tales, stopped publishing altogether, with the verse she continued to produce almost exclusively devotional in nature. Some of her poetry suggests that she was acquainted with the morganatic second wife of Louis XIV, Madame de Maintenon, who provided strong impetus for renewed piety during the final decades of Louis XIV's reign. From all appearances, Bernard was strongly influenced by this atmosphere at the end of her life. She died on 6 September 1712 and was buried in the church of Saint-Paul in Paris.

The two "gallant" tales (*contes galants*) that open *Inès de Cordoue* (1696) are recited by the eponymous heroine, Inès, and her rival, Léonore de Silva, whom Bernard imagines to be among the queen's ladies at the court of Philip II of Spain. The *contes* of both women—Inès's "Le Prince Rosier" ("The Prince Rosebush") and Léonore's "Riquet à la houppe" ("Riquet with the Tuft")—share a number of important similarities.[5] Neither has a known antecedent in oral tradition; both are dystopic; and both prefigure the novel's overriding message that love brings not happiness, but unhappiness. Reflecting an outcome that is anything but stereotypically fairy-tale-like, "Le Prince Rosier" and "Riquet à la houppe" illustrate fully the aesthetic guidelines that are given to Inès and Léonore before they recite their stories: "The adventures should always be implausible, and the emotions always natural," the queen tells her assembled ladies who "judged that these tales were pleasing solely because they showed what happens in the heart and that, furthermore, there was value in the fantasy of imaginations that were not restrained by the appearance of truth" (trans. Seifert).[6] The conjunction of diegetic implausibility and emotional verisimilitude that Bernard proposes here describes the aesthetic of many fairy tales written by seventeenth-century French women writers. Furthermore, by invoking the topos of unhappiness caused by love, Bernard connects her two tales directly to the many contemporaneous French novels, in which this topos was frequent. Even if Bernard contributed relatively little in quantity to the vogue of *contes de fées*, her stylistic and thematic originality makes her significant among the *conteuses*.

Notes

1. Catherine Bernard, *Oeuvres*, ed. Franco Piva, 2 vols. (Fasano; Paris: Schena; Nizet, 1993), 20–21.

2. In his *Parnasse françois* (1732), Titon du Tillet claims, "M. de Fontenelle among others took pleasure in maintaining the bonds of friendship with this Demoiselle (Catherine Bernard) and, with his opinions, helping her in the composition of her works" (trans. Seifert; quoted in Piva, "A la recherche de Catherine Bernard," 25, note 34).

3. Abbé Vertron, *La Nouvelle Pandore ou les Femmes illustres du siècle de Louis le Grand* 2 vols. (Paris: Veuve Maruel, 1698), 2: 363–64.

4. See Piva, "A la recherche de Catherine Bernard," 45–46.

5. Perrault's collection of prose tales also contains a "Riquet à la houppe" that both parallels and differs from Bernard's story. Scholars have attempted to determine which version preceded the other, but there is no convincing proof either way.

6. Bernard, *Oeuvres*, 1: 347–48.

Catherine Bernard's Works

Original Editions

Frédéric de Sicile. Paris: Jean Ribou, 1680.
Les Malheurs de l'amour, Première nouvelle: Éléonor d'Yvrée. Paris: Guerout, 1687.
Le Comte d'Amboise. Paris: Barbin, 1689.
Brutus (staged, 1690). Paris: Veuve de Louis Gontier, 1691.
Histoire de la rupture d'Abenamar et de Fatime. La Haye: N.p., 1696.

Inès de Cordoue, Nouvelle espagnole. [Contains two embedded fairy tales.] Paris: Martin Jouvenel et George Jouvenel, 1696.
Laodamie, Reine d'Epire (staged 1689). Paris: Pierre Ribou, 1735.
Contes. Ed. Raymonde Robert. Paris: Champion, 2005, 279–92.

Modern French Editions of Bernard's Fairy Tales

Bernard, Catherine. *Oeuvres.* Ed. Franco Piva. 2 vols. Fasano; Paris: Schena; Nizet, 1993.
Nouvelles galantes du XVIIe siècle. Ed. Marc Escola. Paris: Garnier-Flammarion, 2004 (*Inès de Cardoue*, 390–449).
Mademoiselle Lhéritier, Mademoiselle Bernard, Mademoiselle de La Force, Madame Durand, Madame D'Auneuil, *Contes.* Ed. Raymonde Robert. Bibliothèque des Génies et des Fées, 2. Paris: Champion, 2005, 273–92.

English Translations

"Riquet with a Tuft." In *The Great Fairy Tale Tradition: From Straparola and Basile to the Brothers Grimm: Texts, Criticism*, ed. and trans. Jack Zipes. New York: Norton, 2001, 717–21.
"Prince Rosebush." In *Enchanted Eloquence: Fairy Tales by Seventeenth-Century Women Writers: The Other Voice in Early Modern Europe*, ed. and trans. Lewis C. Seifert and Domna Stanton. Toronto: Centre for Renaissance and Reformation Studies, forthcoming.

Secondary Literature

Di Scanno, Teresa. "Les Contes de fées de Mademoiselle Bernard ou la vérité psychologique." *Annali Istituto Universitario Orientale* 12 (1970): 261–74.
Ekstein, Nina. "Appropriation and Gender: The Case of Catherine Bernard and Bernard de Fontenelle." *Eighteenth-Century Studies* 30.1 (Fall 1996): 59–80.
Hannon, Patricia. *Fabulous Identities: Women's Fairy Tales in Seventeenth-Century France.* Amsterdam/Atlanta: Rodopi, 1998.
Piva, Franco. "A la recherche de Catherine Bernard." In *Œuvres by Catherine Bernard*, ed. Franco Piva. 2 vols. Fasano; Paris: Schena; Nizet, 1993. 1: 15–47.
Plusquellec, Catherine. *L'OEuvre de Catherine Bernard (Romans, Théâtre, Poésies)*, Thèse de doctorat, Université de Rouen-Haute-Normandie, 1984.
———. "Qui était Catherine Bernard?" *Revue d'Histoire littéraire de la France* 85.4 (1985): 667–69.
Raynard, Sophie. *La Seconde préciosité: Floraison des conteuses de 1690 à 1756.* Biblio 17, 130. Tübingen: Narr Verlag, 2002.

Ringham, Felizitas. "Riquet à la houppe: conteur, conteuse." *French-Studies: A Quarterly Review* 52.3 (1998): 291–304.

Robert, Raymonde. *Le Conte de fées littéraire en France de la fin du XVIIe siècle à la fin du XVIIIe siècle*. [1982] Nancy: Presses universitaires de Nancy, 2002.

Roche-Mazon, Jeanne. *Autour des contes de fées: Recueil d'études de Jeanne Roche-Mazon, accompagnées de pièces complémentaires. Etudes de littérature étrangère et comparée*. Paris: Didier, 1968.

Seifert, Lewis C. *Fairy Tales, Sexuality, and Gender in France, 1690–1715: Nostalgic Utopias*. Cambridge Studies in French, 55. Cambridge: Cambridge University Press, 1996.

Storer, Mary Elizabeth. *Un Episode littéraire de la fin du XVIIe siècle: La Mode des contes de fées (1685–1700)* [1928]; Geneva: Slatkine Reprints, 1972.

Vincent, Monique. "Les Deux versions de Riquet à la houppe: Catherine Bernard (mai 1696), Charles Perrault (octobre 1696)." *Littératures Classiques* 25 (1995): 299–309.

Marie-Jeanne Lhéritier de Villandon

1664–1734

Lewis C. Seifert

Marie-Jeanne Lhéritier de Villandon was born in Paris in 1664, the daughter of Nicholas Lhéritier, one of Louis XIV's official historians, and Françoise Le Clerc, who was either the sister or the niece of Charles Perrault's mother. From all appearances, both Lhéritier's immediate and extended family provided a fertile environment for cultivating literary interests. Her father, in particular, was credited with teaching her Greek and Roman history, mythology, poetry, and tragedy.[1] Lhéritier's brother was a talented mathematician and scientist, and her sister Mademoiselle de Nouvelon published poetry. Lhéritier herself contributed numerous pieces in prose and in verse to the literary magazine *Le Mercure galant*, published three collections of her own writing (which included four fairy tales), edited her patron's memoirs, and translated Ovid's *Heroides*.

If relatively little is known about specific events in Lhéritier's life, we are remarkably well informed about her contacts with contemporaries. Never married, Lhéritier was acquainted with a wide circle of people, including numerous women writers. Her chief patron, the enormously wealthy Duchess of Nemours, was related to many royal families of Europe and was herself sovereign of the principality of Neufchâtel.[2] In 1709, two years after the death of the duchess, Lhéritier published Nemours's memoirs. Lhéritier was also known to the niece of Louis XIV, Mademoiselle d'Orléans, for whom she composed several poems and to whom Perrault dedicated the 1695 manuscript of his *Histoires*. Among the women writers of her time, Lhéritier seems to have been well acquainted with Madeleine de Scudéry (1602–1701), whose salon she is said to have inherited and for whom she wrote *L'Apothéose de Mademoiselle de Scudéry* (1702), a long *éloge* (panegyric) that celebrated not only Scudéry but also many other women writers from antiquity to the seventeenth century. Lhéritier was also familiar with—and perhaps even a close friend of—Antoinette Deshoulières (1637–94), an accomplished poet for whom Lhéritier wrote a posthumous panegyric, *Le Parnasse reconnaissant, ou le Triomphe de Madame Des-Houlières* (1696, *Parnassus Grateful or The Triumph of Madame Des-Houlières*). In these works and others, Lhéritier staunchly defended women's writing against assaults by the likes of Nicolas Boileau, whose virulently misogynist *Satire X* attacked Deshoulières directly. At the same time, Lhéritier, like her uncle, Charles Perrault, was an ardent supporter of the "moderns" in the ongoing Quarrel of the Ancients and the Moderns. In her view, fairy tales—and the Provençal troubadours' lays she purports are their precursors—demonstrate the equivalent value of ancient and modern culture.[3]

Beyond her reputation as a modern and a "champion of the beautiful qualities of the ladies,"[4] Lhéritier earned a measure of literary renown in her day. In 1692 she won a prize from Caen's Académie des Palinots (the Academy of the Palinots). On two occasions, she won prizes from Toulouse's Académie des Lanternistes (the Academy of the Lanternists), to which she was admitted as a member in 1696. A year later, she was granted honorary membership at Padua's Accademia degli Ricovrati (the Academy of the Sheltered). Her salon, which met twice a week, attracted a group of writers and nobles eager to benefit from her critical judgment, according to contemporary sources.[5] Critics have asserted that her fellow *conteuses* d'Aulnoy, Bernard, and Murat attended her salon, although there is only scant evidence to support this claim. In any event, unlike the fairy-tale writers d'Aulnoy, Murat, and La Force, but similar to Bernard, Lhéritier had a reputation for moral rectitude, a reputation that she cultivated throughout her literary work and that she is said to have promoted in her salon.[6] By the time of her death (1734), her renown was such that the austere *Journal des sçavans* devoted a substantial and highly complimentary obituary[7] to her.

Lhéritier's writings provide many valuable insights into the salon storytelling that contributed to the production of *contes de fées* in the 1690s. The three tales in her *Œuvres meslées* (*Various Works*) in 1695 were among the very first of the vogue (only d'Aulnoy and Perrault had published tales before her). In the prefaces to her tales, she alludes to salon conversations about fairy-tale storytelling and mentions the existence of Perrault's collection, which would be published the following year (1697). In "Les Enchantements de l'éloquence" ("The Enchantments of Eloquence"), based on the same source story as Perrault's "Les Fées" ("The Fairies"), there are specific allusions to her uncle's version, which suggests that the two tales may have been written as a sort of friendly competition. In her *Various Works* Lhéritier also refers to Madame de Murat's storytelling, three years before her tales appeared in print. It is clear, then, that Lhéritier was on good terms with both Perrault and Murat and that oral storytelling preceded their published fairy tales.

Throughout the allusions in *Various Works*, Lhéritier affirms that "*contes*" (tales), "*histoires*" (stories), and "*historiettes*" (little stories)—as she calls fairy tales—were parlor games whose ludic function derived from the developments and twists of plot that the storytellers introduced into well-known tales. Overall, though, she places greater emphasis on the didactic purpose of the stories that were told and written. Historically, Lhéritier sees the salon fairy tale as the continuation of a long storytelling tradition that originated with medieval troubadours and that resulted in two offspring, the novel as perpetuated by elite writers and the folktale as practiced by "popular" storytellers.

For their style and form, Lhéritier's tales have often been compared unfavorably to Perrault's more economical stories or d'Aulnoy's less overtly didactic *contes de fées*. While her tales are indeed lengthy and moralistic in tone, they deserve appreciation in their own right. In them, she demonstrates a historical, literary, and rhetorical erudition that is unique among the writers of fairy tales of her time. And in them, she evinces a specific interest in the Middle Ages, a trait that was shared by very few of her contemporaries. Lhéritier should be remembered as one of the very first *conteuses* and as one of the most vocal defenders of the genre. Even if her tales have not always been among the best known of the vogue of late seventeenth-century fairy tales they certainly number among the most interesting, particularly for their portrayal of history and women.

Notes

1. "Eloge de Mademoiselle Lhéritier," *Journal des sçavans* (décembre 1734): 832.

2. The Duchesse de Nemours even invited her protégée to live with her.

3. Marie-Jeanne Lhéritier de Villandon, *Œuvres meslées [. . .] de Mlle L'H**** (Paris: Guignard, 1695). In the concluding moments of the letter that frames her story, "The Enchantment of Eloquence," she writes: "Tales for tales, it seems to me that those from Ancient Gaul are worth just as much as those from Ancient Greece. And Fairies are no less capable of miracles than the Gods of mythology" (*Oeuvres meslées*, 227).

4. Quoted in Storer, 54.

5. Among these are the Marquise de Béthune, the sister of the Queen of Poland (no specific name given), the Princesse de Neufchâtel, the Duchesse de Brisac Béchamel, and Mme de Bellegarde Vertamont ("Eloge de Mademoiselle Lhéritier," 836.)

6. "Eloge de Mademoiselle Lhéritier," 835.

7. The obituary in the *Journal des sçavans* highlights Lhéritier's defense of Deshoulières against Boileau's attack in his Satire X. "Her heroic zeal was applauded by all the admirers of merit," it claims (833). Of Lhéritier's reputation for moral uprightness, the *Journal des sçavans* indicates that she was "exacting for the *bienséances*" and that "she was only connected with those who respected them [the *bienséances*] in all forms. Not only did she detest licentious authors, but satirical writers seemed to her to be the scourge of society" (835).

Marie-Jeanne Lhéritier's Works

Original Editions

Œuvres meslées [. . .] de Mlle L'H***. Paris: Jean Guignard, 1695. [Contains "Les Enchantements de l'éloquence," "Marmoisan, ou l'Innocente tromperie," and "L'Adroite princesse."]

L'Erudition enjouée, ou Nouvelles sçavantes, satyriques et galantes, écrites à une Dame françoise, qui est à Madrid. Paris: Ribou, 1703.

La Tour ténébreuse et les jours lumineux. Paris: Barbin, 1705. [Contains "Ricdin-Ricdon" and "La Robe de sincérité."]

Les Caprices du destin ou Recueil d'histoires singulières et amusantes, arrivées de nos jours. Paris: Huart, 1718.

Les Epîtres héroïques d'Ovide, traduites en vers françois par Mlle L'Héritier. Paris: Prault, 1732.

Modern French Editions of Lhéritier's Fairy Tales

"Les Enchantements de l'éloquence." In *La Fille en garçon*, ed. Catherine Velay-Vallantin. Carcasonne: GARAE/Hésiode, 1992.

Mademoiselle Lhéritier, Mademoiselle Bernard, Mademoiselle de La Force, Madame Durand, Madame D'Auneuil. *Contes*. Ed. Raymonde Robert. Bibliothèque des Génies et des Fées, 2. Paris: Champion, 2005, 17–270.

English Translations of Lhéritier's Fairy Tales

"The Subtle Princess" In *Wonder Tales: Six Stories of Enchantment*, trans. Gilbert Adair, ed. Marina Warner. London: Chatto and Windus, 1994.

"The Discreet Princess, or the Adventures of Finette" (528–42), "The Enchantments of Eloquence" (550–63), "Ricdin-Ricdon" (588–624). In *The Great Fairy Tale Tradition: From Straparola and Basile to the Brothers Grimm: Texts, Criticism*. ed. and trans. Jack Zipes. New York: Norton, 2001.

"Marmoisan." In *Enchanted Eloquence: Fairy Tales by Seventeenth-Century Women Writers*. The Other Voice in Early Modern Europe, ed. and trans. Lewis C. Seifert and Domna Stanton. Toronto: Centre for Renaissance and Reformation Studies, forthcoming.

Secondary Literature

Defrance, Anne. "Les Premiers recueils de contes de fées." *Féeries* 1 (2003): 27–48.

"Eloge de Mademoiselle L'Héritier." *Journal des sçavans* (Décembre 1734): 832–36.

Francillon, Roger. "Une Théorie du folklore à la fin du XVIIe siècle: Mlle Lhéritier." In *Festschrift für Rudolf Schenda zum 65. Geburtstag*, Ursula Brunold-Bigler et al., 205–17. Berne: Lang, 1995.

Fumaroli, Marc. "*Les Fées* de Charles Perrault ou De la littérature." In *Le statut de la littérature: Mélanges offerts à Paul Bénichou*. Geneva: Droz, 1982, 153–86.

Hannon, Patricia. *Fabulous Identities: Women's Fairy Tales in Seventeenth-Century France*. Faux Titre, 151. Amsterdam/Atlanta: Rodopi, 1998.

Jones, Christine. "The Poetics of Enchantment." *Marvels and Tales* 17.1 (2003):55–74.

Mainil, Jean. "'Mes Amies les Fées': Apologie de la femme savante et de la lectrice dans les *Bigarrures ingénieuses* de Marie-Jeanne Lhéritier (1696)." *Féeries* 1 (2003):49–72.

Mercure galant (Mars 1734): 539–40.

Montoya, Alicia C. "Contes du Style des Troubadours: The Memory of the Medieval in Seventeenth-Century French Fairy Tales." In *Medievalism in Technology Old and New*, ed. Karl Fugelso and Carol L. Robinson. Cambridge, UK: Brewer, 2008.

Perrot, Jean. "Dialogisme baroque." *Seventeenth-Century French Studies* 14 (1992): 27–41.

Raynard, Sophie. *La Seconde préciosité: Floraison des conteuses de 1690 à 1756.* Biblio 17, 130. Tübingen: Gunter Narr Verlag, 2002.

Robert, Raymonde. *Le Conte de fées littéraire en France de la fin du XVIIe siècle à la fin du XVIIIe siècle.* [1982] Nancy: Presses universitaires de Nancy, 2002.

———. "L'Insertion des contes merveilleux dans les récits-cadres: Pratique statique, pratique dynamique: *La tour ténébreuse et les jours lumineux* de Mlle Lhéritier, *Les Aventures d'Abdalla* de l'abbé Bignon." *Féeries*1 (2003):73–91.

Seifert, Lewis C. "The Rhetoric of *Invraisemblance*: 'Les enchantements de l'éloquence.'" *Cahiers du Dix-Septième*3.1 (1989):121–39.

———. *Fairy Tales, Sexuality, and Gender in France, 1690–1715: Nostalgic Utopias.* (=Cambridge Studies in French 55. Cambridge: Cambridge University Press, 1996.

Storer, Mary Elizabeth. *Un Episode littéraire de la fin du XVIIe siècle: La mode des contes de fées (1685–1700).* 1928; Geneva: Slatkine Reprints, 1972.

Velay-Vallantin, Catherine. *La Fille en garçon. Classiques de la littérature orale.* Carcassonne: GARAE/Hésiode, 1992.

Vertron, Abbé. *La Nouvelle Pandore ou les Femmes illustres du siècle de Louis le Grand.* 2 vols. Paris: Veuve Maruel, 1698.

Henriette-Julie de Castelnau, Countess de Murat

1668?–1716

Geneviève Patard
(translated and adapted by Sophie Raynard)

Henriette-Julie de Castelnau was born probably in 1668[1] and died in 1716 in Maine.[2] Both her grandfathers were marshals of France and belonged to the high aristocracy. Her father, Michel de Castelnau, was from Bigorre, and her mother, Louise-Marie Foucault, was from Limousin. Henriette's alliance with Nicolas de Murat, Count de Gilbertez, a colonel of an infantry regiment, was an equally prestigious match. Henriette's father, who was the governor of Brest, died on 2 December 1672, from a wound he had previously received near Utrecht in Holland. From that point forward, her family can be documented in Paris from the well-known correspondence of Marie de Rabutin-Chantal, Marquise de Sévigné,[3] with whom she and her family were closely acquainted. The long-held belief that Murat spent her youth in Brittany originated in 1818, when the Breton Miorcec de Kerdanet wrote that Henriette-Julie spent her early years in Brittany before coming to Paris at the age of sixteen, where to everyone's admiration she was introduced to the queen in 1686 dressed in a Breton costume. The French literary historian Edouard Guitton suspects that the myth was based on Voltaire's *Ingénu* (1767), with its similarly picturesque scene as the heroine Mademoiselle de Saint-Yves arrives in Versailles from her native Brittany and fascinates all observers. According to Guitton this kind of fiction was designed to conceal a far less edifying reality. Whatever the reason, it was energetically spread by nineteenth-century biographers and generally accepted by twentieth-century scholars.

Scandalous rumors that swirled around Murat in the 1690s and the first years of the 1700s culminated in her 1702 exile to Loches. Nineteenth- and twentieth-century biographers disagree on the reasons for her banishment as well as on the chronology of events. The biographical note written by Evrard Titon du Tillet sixteen years after Murat's death remains discrete: "The vivaciousness of her spirit and her taste for pleasure raised rumors on several occasions however ill founded they might have been."[4] One wonders if he based his statement on Murat's *Mémoires* (*Memoirs*), which she undertook to "defend the ladies," whom she claimed were so often, and wrongly, maligned. In the late eighteenth century, Joseph Mayer, editor of the *Cabinet des fées* (*The Chamber of the Fairies*), stated that Françoise d'Aubigné, Marquise de Maintenon (Louis XIV's morganatic second wife) had accused the countess of authoring a pamphlet against Louis XIV and his entourage, an offence that caused her to be exiled in 1694. The pamphlet has never been identified, however, and the date is questionable, since her presence in Paris's elevated literary circles through the 1690s is attested by testimony both direct and indirect. For instance, Marie-Jeanne Lhéritier dedicated "L'Adroite Princesse" ("The Subtle Princess") to her in 1696; and two years later Claude-Charles Guyonnet de Vertron dedicated a madrigal to her which placed her among "the illustrious women of Louis XIV's century"; while the contemporary scholar Roger Marchal[5] mentions that Murat frequented the salon of Anne-Thérèse de Marguenat de Courcelles, Marquise de Lambert, which opened in 1692 in the very heart of Paris in the rue de Richelieu. In addition, Murat was elected to the Accademia degli Ricovrati (Academy of the Sheltered) in 1699, along with Charlotte-Rose de la Force and Catherine Bernard, joining fellow *conteuses* who had been received into membership: Marie-Catherine d'Aulnoy and Marie-Jeanne Lhéritier, as well as Madeleine de Scudéry and Antoinette Deshoulières in the early 1680s.

All currently available evidence points toward a single conclusion: Murat wrote her 1690s works from Paris and not from a forced rustication in Touraine 180 miles southwest of Paris in the castle of Loches. Her 1690s residence in Paris agrees with the social dimension of the fairy-tale vogue, which spread within the sophisticated sphere between Paris and Versailles.

Murat published most of her oeuvre between 1697 and 1699: her *Mémoires* (Memoirs) appeared in 1697, her two collections of fairy tales *Contes de Fées* (Fairy Tales) and *Les Nouveaux Contes des Fées* (New Fairy Tales or New Tales of the Fairies) in 1698, her *Histoires sublimes et allégoriques* (Sublime and Allegorical Stories) with four fairy tales in 1699, and her *Voyage de Campagne* (Country Diary) with its ghost stories and one fairy tale in 1699.

From this point forward Murat's life, like that of her fellow *conteuse* Marie-Catherine d'Aulnoy, reads like a scandalous novel. Historical documents from 1698 and the following years—the administrative correspondence of Jérôme Phélypeaux, Count de Pontchartrain's[6] and the police reports[7] of René d'Argenson[8]—contradict traditionally presented reasons for Murat's exile and illuminate relevant dates. They clarify "Madame de Murat's disorders," namely, her lesbianism,[9] while the dating of other correspondence[10] reveals the timing of her arrest and her removal to the castle of Loches.[11]

Pontchartrain's administrative correspondence also traces Murat's life from 1702 to 1706. Two letters addressed to the king's lieutenant in Loches, for instance, specify the conditions of her detention, which included the payment of her pension, the granting of certain liberties so that the countess might "go outdoors and avoid boredom," vigilance concerning the men but also the "women and girls" whom she might see, and finally the surveillance of her correspondence. Complementary documentation from 1703 and 1704 reveals her efforts to recover freedom in the same period. After a failed escape on 14 March 1706 she was transferred to the castle prison of Saumur[12] and subjected to stricter rules. She spent a brief period of time in the Angers castle prison in 1707 before being returned to Loches later that year.

Two years later Murat addressed the Duke d'Orléans through his mistress, the Countess d'Argenton, to whom she had dedicated a poem, and obtained a quasifreedom on 15 May 1709. Banishment continued, however, since her freedom was conditional on her remaining far distant from Paris at the home of an aunt in Limousin.

In those years she published nothing, contenting herself with correspondence and a journal.[13] Largely unpublished, these texts express bitterness at her exile and suffering from loneliness and illness. Manuscript letters from 1708 and 1709 addressed to her cousin Mademoiselle de Menou relate small events in the city of Loches and record her writing of verses, songs, and tales. In 1709 Murat composed her last book, *Les Lutins du château de Kernosy* (The Elves of Kernosy Castle, 1710), a frametale narrative that takes place in Brittany in a remote castle that is haunted by ghosts. There guests of the young Kernosy ladies tell a range of elf stories and create a fantastic and haunting atmosphere.

Little is known about the last years of Madame de Murat's life. Even though the Duke d'Orléans had restored complete freedom to her by allowing her to return to Paris, she was unwell and retired to La Buzardière, her paternal grandmother's castle in Maine. She fell into oblivion, and—weak and unwell—she died there on 29 September 1716.

Madame de Murat's life, split between the effervescence of urban sophistication and the solitary confinement of her years of enforced retirement, has produced polarly opposed depictions of her and her life. René d'Argenson's reports describe a diabolic creature; her *Memoirs* portray a virtuous victim. In theoretical terms her memoires represent a defense and vindication of women's cause, in the form of a response to a book attributed to Saint-Évremont that was, according to the countess, likely to insinuate "a very disadvantageous opinion on women." Her memoires thus used her life to justify the rights of women in an ongoing debate about gender. A more realistic image is probably that of a free woman refusing masculine violence and fighting for the recognition of her sex.

Notes

1. According to Frédéric Lemeunier's investigation based on original documents from La Buzardière's archives.

2. *Nouveau Mercure Galant*, Octobre 1716, 228.

3. Madame de Sévigné, *Lettres*, ed. Roger Duchêne, 3 vols. (Paris: Gallimard, Pléiade, 1972–78). Letters from 16 mai 1672 (1: 513); 5 janvier 1674 (1: 656); 12 août 1675 (2: 52); 10 janvier 1689 (3: 467).

4. Titon du Tillet, *Le Parnasse françois* (Paris: J. B. Coignard, 1732), 562.

5. "In its first period, Madame de Lambert's salon reserved the warmest welcome to the feminine novel and its authors: Madame d'Aulnoy [. . .], Catherine Bernard, the Countess de Murat, Mademoiselle de La Force; and the Présidente Ferrand must have undoubtedly adorned it as well for he had witnessed the blossoming of the short-story's masterpieces." In Roger Marchal, *Madame de Lambert et son milieu.* (Oxford: The Voltaire Foundation, 1991), 226.

6. Jérôme Phélypeaux (March 1674–78 February 1747), Comte de Pontchartrain, served as as a councillor to the Parliament of Paris from 1692, and served with his father as secretary of state of the Maison du Roi and navy minister from 1699 onwards.

7. One can read this in the 24 February 1700 report: "The crimes that are attributed to Madame de Murat are not of a kind to be easily proven by way of information, because they deal with domestic impiety and a monstrous attachment to people of her own sex. However I would very much like to know

what she would say to the following facts: a portrait pierced several times with a knife, an act caused by her jealousy towards a woman she loved and then left a few months ago only to become attached to Madame de Nantiat, another woman of the greatest dissoluteness, known less for the fines she incurred for her gambling than for her moral disorder. That woman, who is housed by [Murat], is the object of her perpetual adorations, even in the presence of some valets and pawnbrokers." A little later: "Madame de Murat and her accomplices are so dreaded in the neighborhood, that no one dares expose oneself to their vengeance."

8. Marc-René de Voyer de Paulmy d'Argenson (1652–1721) was minister and lieutenant-general of police for twenty-one years, from 1697 to 1718.

9. Louis XIV loathed homosexuality.

10. In d'Argenson: letter dated 19 April 1702, from Pontchartrain to the Marshal de Boufflers, Murat's godfather.

11. Town located in the department of Indre-et-Loire, which some sometimes confused with the town of Auch. Loches possesses a powerful citadel that Louis XIV used as a state prison.

12. So she mentions in her *Journal*.

13. *Journal*, Bibliothèque de l'Arsenal (MS 3471).

Henriette-Julie de Murat's Works

Memoirs

Mémoires de madame la comtesse de M***. 2 vols. Paris: Claude Barbin, 1697.

Fairy Tales

Contes de Fées. *Dédiez à Son Altesse Sérénissime Madame la Princesse Douairière de Conty. Par Mad. La Comtesse de M****. Paris: Claude Barbin, 1698. [Includes "Le Parfait Amour," "Anguillette," and "Jeune et Belle."]

Les Nouveaux Contes des Fées. Par Madame de M***. Paris: Claude Barbin, 1698 (2nd ed. 1710). [Includes "Le Palais de la Vengeance," "Le Prince des Feuilles," and "L'Heureuse Peine."]

Histoires sublimes et allégoriques. Par Madame la Comtesse D**. Dédiées aux Fées Modernes. Paris: Florentin et Pierre Delaulne, 1699. [Includes "Le Roi Porc," "L'Île de la Magnificence," "Le Sauvage," and "Le Turbot."]

Madame de Murat. Conte,. ed. Geneviève Patard. Paris: Champion, 2006.

Narratives

Voyage de campagne. Par Madame la Comtesse de M***. 2 vols. Paris: Veuve de Claude Barbin, 1699. [Includes "Conte du Père et de ses quatre fils."]

Les Lutins du château de Kernosy, nouvelle historique. Par Madame la Comtesse de M***. Paris: Jacques Le Febvre, 1710.

Unpublished (Miscellaneous Pieces)

MS 3471 de la Bibliothèque de l'Arsenal (Paris), "Ouvrages de Mme la C. de Murat, journal pour Mademoiselle de Menou" (1708). [Includes "L'Aigle au beau bec," "La Fée Princesse," and "Peine Perdue."]

Cromer, Sylvie. *Édition du Journal pour Mademoiselle de Menou, d'après le Manuscrit 3471 de la Bibliothèque de l'Arsenal: Ouvrages de Mme la Comtesse de Murat.* Thèse de 3e cycle, Sorbonne, 1984.

Secondary Literature

Barchilon, Jacques. *Le Conte merveilleux français de 1690 à 1790: Cent ans de féerie et de poésie ignorées de l'histoire littéraire.* Paris: Champion, 1975.

Boulay de la Meurthe, Alfred. "Les prisonniers du roi à Loches sous Louis XIV." *Bulletin et mémoires de la société archéologique de Touraine* 49 (1910): 1–119.

Correspondance administrative sous le règne de Louis XIV, ed. Georges Bernard Depping. Vol. 2. Paris: Imprimerie nationale, 1850–55.

Démoris, René. *Le Roman à la première personne. Du Classicisme aux Lumières.* Paris: A. Colin, 1975. 281–86

Genieys-Kirk, Séverine. "Narrating the Self in Mme de Murat's Mémoires de Madame la Comtesse de M*** avant sa retraite. Servant de réponse aux Mémoires de Mr. Evremond (1697)." In *Narrating the Self in Early Modern Europe. L'Écriture de soi dans l'Europe moderne*, ed. Bruno Tribout et Ruth Wheland. Oxford and New York: Peter Lang (European Connections), 2007. 161–76.

Guitton, Edouard. "Madame de Murat ou la fausse ingénue." *Études creusoises* 8 (1987): 203–6.

Hipp, Marie-Thérèse. *Mythes et réalité. Enquête sur le roman et les mémoires.* Paris: Klincksieck, 1976. 309–17.

Miorcec de Kerdanet, Daniel-Louis. *Notices chronologiques sur les théologiens, jurisconsultes, philosophes, artistes, littérateurs . . . de la Bretagne, depuis le commencement de l'ère chrétienne jusqu'à nos jours.* Brest: Michel, 1818.

Patard, Geneviève. "Murat, Henriette-Julie de Castelnau, comtesse de" http://www.siefar.org/DicoA-Z.html (2007).

Rapports inédits du lieutenant de police René d'Argenson (1697–1715), ed. Paul Cottin. Paris: Plon, 1891.

Rivara, Annie. "*Le Voyage de campagne* comme machine à produire et à détruire des contes d'esprits." In *Le Conte merveilleux au XVIIIe siècle. Une poétique expérimentale*, ed. Régine Jomand-Baudry and Jean-François Perrin. Paris: Kimé, 2002. 353–69.

Robert, Raymonde. *Le Conte de fées littéraire en France de la fin du XVIIe à la fin du XVIIIe siècle* avec Supplément bibliographique 1980–2000. Paris: Champion, 2002.

Robinson, David Michael. "The Abominable Madame de Murat." In *Homosexuality in French History and Culture*, ed. Jeffrey Merrick and Michael Sibalis. Philadelphia: Harrington Park, 2001. 53–67.

Ségalen, Auguste-Pierre. "Madame de Murat et le Limousin." In *Le Limousin au XVIIe siècle: littérature, histoire, histoire religieuse* (colloque de Limoges 9–10 oct. 1976). Limoges: Trames, 1979.

Sermain, Jean-Paul. *Métafictions. La Réflexivité dans la littérature d'imagination (1670–1730).* (Les Dix-huitièmes siècles 65). Paris: Champion, 2002.

———. Le Conte de fées du classicisme aux Lumières. Paris: Desjonquères, 2005.

Storer, Mary Elizabeth. *Un Épisode littéraire de la fin du XVIIe siècle: la mode des contes de fées (1685–1700).* [1928]; Geneva: Slatkine Reprints, 1972.

Charlotte-Rose de Caumont de La Force

1650?–1724

Lewis C. Seifert

Charlotte-Rose de Caumont de La Force was born, probably in 1650, to an illustrious and highly placed aristocratic family that included writers and generals. On her mother's side she was related to the *conteuse* Henriette-Julie de Murat. As Protestants, La Force's family had been actively involved in the Wars of Religion during the sixteenth century. At the time of the revocation of the Edict of Nantes, however, she converted to Catholicism, an act all the more necessary since she frequented court circles and was known personally to Louis XIV. The king accorded her an annual pension and named her *fille d'honneur* (maid of honor) to several women at court, including the dauphine (the wife of the heir to the throne). In this capacity, she frequented court festivities, was mentioned in contemporary accounts of Louis XIV's reign,[1] and was intimately acquainted with many people at court.

In spite of royal favor, La Force's reputation was touched by scandal. In her role as *fille d'honneur* of the dauphine, for example, she was accused of misconduct, including possession of a pornographic novel.[2] She was also rumored to have had love affairs, which are fictionalized in a novel of the time.[3]

In 1687, La Force married Charles de Briou, but without the permission of his father, who immediately sought an annulment. After a lengthy trial that attracted the scandalmongers of the day, La Force's marriage was indeed annulled in 1689. In 1697, La Force was accused of authoring satirical songs, a scandal of a more serious nature, and Louis XIV banished her from both court and Paris. She retired to a convent in Gercy where she stayed for the next sixteen years and where she is thought to have composed at least two novels and numerous poems.[4] In an autobiography written perhaps during this period, La Force exhibits a remarkable self-awareness, admitting to ambition, independence, and a penchant for glory and love.[5] Little is known about the final years of La Force's life apart from her difficult financial circumstances. She died in 1724.

In her time, La Force's literary fortune was considerably better than her personal reputation. The *Mercure galant*, a seventeenth-century literary magazine, praised her works on several occasions and, in 1685, declared that "she has always been considered to be the arbiter of works of the mind."[6] Her historical novels were widely appreciated and republished well into the eighteenth century.

Like several of her fellow women fairy-tale writers, she was an honorary member of Padua's Accademia degli Ricovrati (The Academy of the Sheltered). From poems that were addressed to her, it is clear that she had contact with numerous writers of her day, including Antoinette Deshoulières and Antoine Hamilton.[7] Less clear is the interaction she may have had with other *conteuses* and *conteurs* before her 1697 banishment. In any event, we know that La Force shared her tales with acquaintances before publishing them.[8]

La Force's writing incorporates many conventions of late seventeenth-century prose fiction, particularly those of the "secret history" genre. Nonetheless, her work is characterized by sophisticated techniques, such as multiple embedded stories and narrative points of view (similar to many other fairy tales by women at the time). La Force's *Contes des contes* (*Tales of the Tales*) presents an idealized vision of love and thinly disguised descriptions of court settings; the stories also reveal a thorough knowledge of mythology and existing literary fairy tales.[9] Several of her tales display a mild eroticism that was unusual for the period, although it appears restrained by later standards. Several of her tales are regularly translated and republished, including "Persinette" (a version of "Rapunzel"), "Plus Belle que Fée" ("Fairer Than a Fairy"), and "La Bonne Femme" ("The Good Woman").

Notes

1. See, for instance, Philippe de Courcillon de Dangeau, et al., *Journal du marquis de Dangeau* (Biographical Sources) who documents (albeit in passing)

her rise to favor at court. See, in particular, his entries for 8 July, 21 September, and 26 November 1686; 7 June and 8 December 1687; 17 January, 18 January, and 30 January 1688; 15 July 1689; and 15 February 1697.

2. See the Princess Palatine's letter of 28 October 1687 (Charlotte-Elisabeth d'Orléans, *Lettres de Madame, Duchesse d'Orléans, née Princesse Palatine*, ed. Olivier Amiel (Paris: Mercure de France, 1985), 109–11.

3. See Storer, 112. In her letter of 28 October 1687, the Princess Palatine reports that the governess of the Dauphine's *filles d'honneur* had found in their possession a "book filled with so many ignominious things that every single chapter speaks of the most horrible positions one can imagine" (see *Lettres de Madame, Duchesse d'Orléans*, 110) and recounts the angry response this news provoked in both Madame de Maintenon and Louis XIV. At the end of this letter, La Force is specifically mentioned as one of the *filles d'honneur* involved in the scandal (111).

4. Charlotte Rose de Caumont de La Force, *Les Jeux d'esprit ou, la promenade de la Princesse de Conti à Eu*, ed. M. le Marquis de La Grange (Paris: A. Aubry, 1862),xxv.

5. Ibid., xx–xxiv.

6. Ibid., xv.

7. See the poem Hamilton dedicated to her in Storer, 111–12. Hamilton enjoins La Force to "spend in innocence, relaxation, and ease / What remains of [their] tranquil days." He also expresses the hope that they will once again see each other at the Hôtel de Vilgagnon, where they can share pâté, champagne, ham, and songs.

8. Simon Benard, the publisher of La Force's *Contes des contes*, states that her collection had been completed well before publication and that it had received "the approbation of persons of quality." See Charlotte-Rose de Caumont de La Force, *Les Contes des contes* (Paris: Simon Benard, 1697),preface.

9. The title of La Force's collection—*Les Contes des contes*—recalls Basile's *Lo Cunto de li cunti (Tale of Tales)*. The date of publication of her volume is given as 23 December 1697, while Perrault's volume bears an earlier date, in the spring 1697.

Charlotte-Rose de La Force's Works

Original Editions

Histoire secrète de Bourgogne. Paris: Simon Benard, 1694.
Histoire secrète de Henry IV, roy de Castille. Paris: Simon Benard, 1695.
Histoire de Marguerite de Valois, reine de Navarre, sœur de François Ier. Paris: Simon Benard, 1696.
Les Contes des contes. Paris: Simon Benard, 1697. [Includes "Plus Belle que Fée," "Persinette," "L'Enchanteur," "Tourbillon," "Vert et Bleu," "Les Pays des Délices," "La Puissance d'Amour," and "La Bonne Femme."]

Gustave Vasa, histoire de Suède. Paris: Simon Benard, 1697⁻98.

Anecdote galante, ou Histoire secrète de Catherine de Bourbon, duchesse de Bar, et sœur de Henry le Grand. Nancy: s.p., 1703.

Les Jeux d'esprit, ou La Promenade de la princesse de Conty à Eu. Ed. le marquis de La Grange. Paris: Aubry, 1862.

Modern French Editions

Les Fées, Contes des contes. Vol. 7 of *Nouveau cabinet des fées*. Geneva: Slatkine Reprints, 1978.

"Plus Belle que Fée," "Persinette," and "Tourbillon." In *Le Cabinet des fées*. Ed. Elizabeth Lemirre. Arles: Picquier, 1994. 2: 9–57.

Mademoiselle Lhéritier, Mademoiselle Bernard, Mademoiselle de La Force, Madame Durand, Madame D'Auneuil, *Contes*. Ed. Raymonde Robert. Bibliothèque des Génies et des Fées, 2. Paris: Champion, 2005. 295⁻434.

English Translations

"Persinette." Jack Zipes, ed. and trans. *The Great Fairy Tale Tradition: From Straparola and Basile to the Brothers Grimm: Texts, Criticism*. New York: W.W. Norton, 2001. 479⁻84.

"The Enchanter" and "Green and Blue." Lewis C. Seifert and Domna Stanton, ed. and trans. *Enchanted Eloquence: Fairy Tales by Seventeenth-Century Women Writers. The Other Voice in Early Modern Europe* (Toronto: Centre for Renaissance and Reformation Studies, forthcoming).

Secondary Literature

Barchilon, Jacques. "'L'Enchanteur': Un conte de Mlle de la Force." *Marvels and Tales* 2.1 (1998): 47⁻60.

Dangeau, Philippe de Courcillon de. *Journal du marquis de Dangeau*. Ed. Eudoxe Soulié, et al. Paris: Firmin Didot frères, 1854.

Dubos, Jean-Baptiste. *La Correspondance de l'abbé Du Bos (1670⁻1742)*. Ed. Alfred Lombard. Genève: Slatkine Reprints, 1969.

Hannon, Patricia. *Fabulous Identities: Women's Fairy Tales in Seventeenth-Century France*. Amsterdam. Atlanta: Rodopi, 1998.

Legault, Marianne. "Au-dela du miroir: Le Merveilleux féminin dans l'univers du conte de La Force." Actes du 33ᵉ congrès annuel de la North American Society for Seventeenth-Century French Literature, III, Arizona State University (Tempe) May 2001. Ed. David Wetsel, et al. Tubingen: Narr, 2003. 277⁻87.

———. *Narrations déviantes: L'intimité entre femmes dans l'imaginaire français du dix-septième siècle*. Québec: Les Presses de l'université Laval, 2008.

Jacobs, Eva. "Anthony Hamilton et Mademoiselle de La Force." *Revue des Sciences Humaines* 115 (1964): 379-90.

Maistre-Welch, Marcelle. "L'Eros féminin dans les contes de fées de Mlle de la Force." *Actes du XXIIe colloque de la North American Society for Seventeenth-Century French Literature, Univ. of Nevada, Las Vegas (1-3 mars 1990).* Ed. Marie-France Hilgar. Tübingen / Seattle / Paris: Papers on French Seventeenth Century Literature, 1991. 217-23.

Orléans, Charlotte-Elisabeth (d'). *Lettres de Madame, duchesse d'Orléans, née Princesse Palatine.* Ed. Olivier Amiel. Paris: Mercure de France, 1985.

Raynard, Sophie. *La Seconde préciosité: Floraison des conteuses de 1690 à 1756.* Biblio 17, 130. Tübingen: Gunter Narr, 2002.

Robert, Raymonde. *Le Conte de fées littéraire en France de la fin du XVIIe siècle à la fin du XVIIIe siècle.* [1982] Nancy: Presses universitaires de Nancy, 2002.

Seifert, Lewis C. *Fairy Tales, Sexuality, and Gender in France, 1690-1715: Nostalgic Utopias.* Cambridge Studies in French, 55. Cambridge: Cambridge University Press, 1996.

Storer, Mary Elizabeth. *Un Episode littéraire de la fin du XVIIe siècle: La Mode des contes de fées (1685-1700)* [1928]. Geneva: Slatkine Reprints, 1972.

Thirard, Marie-Agnès. "Les Contes de Mlle de la Force: Un nouvel art du récit féerique à travers un exemple privilégié." *Papers on French Seventeenth Century Literature* 27.53 (2000): 573-85.

Tucker, Holly. "Like Mother, Like Daughter: Maternal Cravings and Birthmarks in the Fairy Tales of Mme d'Aulnoy and Mlle de la Force." *The Mother in/and French Literature.* Ed. Buford Norman. Amsterdam: Rodopi, 2000. 33-50.

Vellenga, Carolyn. "Rapunzel's Desire: A Reading of Mlle de la Force." *Merveilles et Contes* 6.1 (1992): 103-16.

III

Exoticism

Galland
Eighteenth-Century France

Antoine Galland

1646–1715

Manuel Couvreur
(translated and adapted by Sophie Raynard)

Antoine Galland's literary career, without being unique, constitutes a spectacular exception among the professional writers the emergence of whom Alain Viala analyzed in his classic work.[1] First, as a man from a modest background, Galland had to pursue literature primarily as a source of revenue. He was faced with two options. On the one hand, he could pursue a career as a writer in the modern sense of the word, relying on highly placed support and hoping to gain recognition from such authorities as the French Academy. On the other hand, he could follow a less brilliant but also less risky career based on an objective body of expertise. Galland opted for the latter and became a scholar of Middle Eastern languages, a choice that allowed him to earn a living as a librarian and a preceptor. He was also able to obtain some recognition, the most glorious manifestation of which (in his eyes) was his nomination to the Collège Royal.

Paradoxically for his atypical career, Galland eventually achieved an exceptional literary recognition: his version of *The Thousand and One Nights* was without a doubt one of the most translated and read French books in eighteenth-century Europe. Equally paradoxical in literary history is that his renown derived not, strictly speaking, from a translation, because Galland's translation was not simply a transposition from one language to another, but from a re-creation, whose style Proust used as one of his points of reference and some of whose narrative content (that is, a large part of some of the most famous tales) came from Galland's own imagination.

Antoine Galland was born in Rollot in the Department of Somme on 6 April 1646. As he later wrote, he was the youngest of a family of seven that was "poor but spotless and irreproachable."[2] At his father's death in 1650 his mother "did not go against but even indulged his inclination for literature."[3] His exceptional intellectual capacities blossomed at the Collège de Noyon, where he studied Latin, Greek, and Hebrew. For a poor and gifted child like the young Galland, an ecclesiastical career could have led to social elevation. But Galland, unlike so many of his contemporaries, refused to utter vows that would not have been sincere. His mother then "determined to have him learn a trade." In the end however his taste for literature won the day, and Galland left for Paris.

On his arrival in Paris in September 1661, a recommendation to Nicolas Bouthillier, assistant principal at the Collège Duplessis, opened the doors of that institution to him. Although his aptitudes allowed him to enter the tenth grade directly, he later could not afford to print his dissertation and therefore could not defend the work that would have given him the degree of Master of Arts. Remaining in Paris, he deepened his knowledge of Latin and pursued his studies of ancient Greek on his own initiative. At the same time, he attended classes in Arabic and Hebrew at the Collège Royal, studying with Pierre Vattier and Valérien de Flavigny, respectively. His demonstrated capabilities gained him a place on the Royal Rewards list of 10 March 1666.

It is likely that the same Bouthillier who had helped Galland at the Collège Duplessis interceded to help him become the secretary and librarian for Nicolas Petitpied. Petitpied, close to the milieus of Port-Royal, introduced him to famous Jansenists such as Antoine Arnauld and Pierre Nicole, who in their turn recommended him to the Marquis of Nointel, who had recently been appointed French ambassador to Constantinople. With Nointel, Galland embarked for Turkey on 22 August 1670.

In Turkey, working on behalf of Nointel, Louis XIV and his prime minister, Jean-Baptiste Colbert, Galland purchased ancient Greek and Roman artifacts as well as Arabic, Turkish, and Persian artifacts and manuscripts. Such activity prompted him to deepen his knowledge of these peoples, their histories, their languages, and their literatures. In that large frame of reference, he sought the acquaintance of everyone who could help him, be it the renegade Haly-Beg[4] or European travelers such as Guillaume-Joseph Grelot,[5] Jean Chardin,[6] Laurent d'Arvieux,[7] Cornelio Magni,[8] Thomas Smith,[9] John Covel,[10] or Sir Paul Rycaut.[11]

After endless negotiations, Ambassador Nointel obtained in August 1673 the ratification of new commercial agreements between France and the Ottoman Empire. To celebrate that diplomatic success, Nointel treated himself—at the king's expense—to a lavish journey that took him to Egypt, Jerusalem, Athens, and finally Smyrna for over a year (from September 1673 to January 1675), during which Galland accompanied him. However, when Louis XIV learned how extravagant his ambassador had been, Nointel fell into disgrace, and Galland discreetly returned to France without showing any type of support for his former patron.

Back in Paris in 1675 scholars sought out Galland. He met Henry Justel and became acquainted with Ismaël Bouilliau, Melchisédech Thévenot, and Pierre-Daniel Huet.[12] Another acquaintance, Jean Gallois, attended the Academy of Caen, which in its turn was directly attached to Paris academies, such as the Academy of Medals and the French Academy. Through a correspondence, Galland established contacts with Sir George Wheeler[13] and especially Jacob Spon.[14] In 1678 the famous Paris publisher Claude Barbin agreed to publish the young antiquarian's first book, *La Mort du sultan Osman* (The Death of Sultan Oman), a great success, as the subsequent composition of two pirated editions attests. Thenceforward, Galland presented himself as a translator and mediator of Oriental culture to French readers.

Galland's reputation was becoming firmly established, but his financial situation remained precarious until a certain Giraud from Lyon and Jean Foy Vaillant, then considered the top numismatist in France, provided him with an allowance so that he could undertake a second journey to the Middle East. On 8 March 1678 he debarked in Smyrna where he remained for a few months. Galland returned from his second journey in September 1678, bringing with him his *Smyrne ancienne et moderne* (Ancient and Modern Smyrna). It was to have been published by Barbin, but the publisher requested changes that Galland categorically refused. That was the first of many disagreements between the uncompromising Galland and the less scrupulous Barbin.

Galland left again in January 1679 for a third journey to the East. Hired by the Levant Company, he traveled to Constantinople with the newly installed French ambassador to Turkey, the Marquis de

Guilleragues, a fine literateur and author of the famous *Lettres portugaises* (Portuguese Letters). A privileged relationship developed between the two men. Galland traveled through the Turkish archipelago, stayed for five years in Constantinople, and continued to purchase artifacts for the royal collections.

After the deaths of Jean-Baptiste Colbert (1683) and Guilleragues (1685) Galland's financial situation became perilous, although his renown gained him admission to Padua's Accademia degli Ricovrati (The Academy of the Sheltered). On 1 September 1685, however, he was appointed "the king's antiquarian" with a modest salary. Returning to Turkey from Egypt in 1688, Galland was caught in a terrible earthquake, which completely destroyed the city of Smyrna. Rescued from the debris uninjured, Galland returned permanently to France in December 1688.

The decade that Galland had spent in the East had allowed him to perfect his knowledge of the cultures and languages of the eastern Mediterranean, especially of ancient and modern Greek, Turkish, Arabic, Persian, Syriac, and Hebrew. Competent, but poor, Galland put himself at the service of wealthy orientalists as secretary, librarian, and translator. He served, respectively, Melchisédech Thévenot, the keeper of the king's library, until his death in 1692, and later, Barthélemy d'Herbelot, whose famous *Bibliothèque orientale* (Oriental Library) Galland helped prepare, and which he published posthumously after Herbelot's death. Although recognized and respected by his peers, Galland was not selected to succeed Herbelot as Chair of Syriac at the Collège Royal, so he entered the service of Thierry Bignon,[15] remaining in his employ until Bignon's death in 1697. For the following twelve years, Galland served Nicolas-Joseph Foucauld, the intendent of Lower Normandy, whom he accompanied to the city of Caen.

During his sojourn in Caen Galland was particularly acquainted with Gilles Ménage and Jean Regnaud de Segrais, two of the leading theoreticians of the novel. In 1694 Galland published a well-received selection of *Paroles remarquables, bons mots et maximes des Orientaux* (Remarkable Sayings, Bons Mots, and Maxims from the Orientals). That book reveals how concerned Galland was to establish a connection between the genres in vogue in France and foreign models of the same genres, which he held to be equally admirable and undeniably more ancient. The *Paroles remarquables* follow the tradition of both the *iana*[16] genre—which Galland had enriched with *Ménagiana* (1693) and *Segraisiana* (published posthumously in 1721)—and the maxim, a genre that François de La Rochefoucauld in particular had exemplified. Jean de La Fontaine, in the last volumes of his *Fables*, had been inspired principally by Bidpai[17] wisdom tales whose apologues had been revealed to him by Gilbert Gaulmin's[18] translation. In 1696 Galland proposed a new Bidpai translation to Barbin, one based not on Persian sources but on a Turkish manuscript. But because Galland refused once again to accommodate Barbin's conditions, his project floundered, and it was only in 1724 that Thomas-Simon Gueullette published Galland's manuscript with minor changes. With six levels of embedded narratives, Galland's manuscript presented a construction close to that of the future *Thousand and One Nights*. *Les Fables indiennes, politiques et morales* (Bidpai's Indian Political and Moral Fables) intended to enlighten kings on ruling their kingdoms, comprised a large number of parable-like narratives that illustrate the necessary balance between the ideal of ataraxia—symbolized by the desert and the retreat—and ambition—represented by the quest and the journey. The book also explored the question of the generic proximity between the fable and the tale.

In 1706, back in Paris, Galland served in the Academy of Inscriptions and Medals, in which Perrault had served twenty-some years earlier. In 1709 he was finally appointed Chair of Arabic at the Collège Royal. In 1712 he was invited to accept responsibility for the *Cabinet des médailles* (the medal collection), but he declined this prestigious offer: "I was not likely to present myself every day before his majesty when he woke up in the crowd of his courtiers; moreover, I had to take into account the obligation of living in Versailles, in some kind of slavery."[19] If we may rely on the Abbé de Louvois's account of his surprising response, Louis XIV, far from taking offence, could not keep himself from admiring Galland for his refusal. Galland died in Paris on 17 February 1715.

Galland's tardy recognition was due more to the enormous social success conferred by *The Thousand and One Nights* than to his long-evident scholarly reputation. Galland had undertaken the translation of Sindbad's travels by 1696, but at the moment in which it was to be published, he discovered that the Sindbad tale cycle was but one segment of "a prodigious collection of similar tales entitled *The Thousand and One Nights*,"[20] a popular book then totally unknown either to European or to Middle Eastern scholars. In October 1701 Galland asked friends traveling in the East to send him a copy of that text; the manuscript that he received remains extraordinarily precious because of its great age and coherent nature. At the beginning of 1702 Galland began to translate it to "entertain himself on long evenings."[21]

Dedicated to the "Marquise of O," the Marquis de Guilleragues' daughter, *The Thousand and One Nights* began being published in Paris by Barbin's widow (la Veuve Barbin) in 1704. Once again, Galland connected a translation to a literary genre then in vogue, namely, the fairy tale. In his eyes, the Arabic collection was unequaled among existing fairy tales: "Nothing more beautiful has been seen so far, in any language."[22] As for the marvelous, the reader was asked to judge "how much the Arabs surpass[ed] other nations in that sort of composition." The book went beyond French *contes de fées* in its ingenious structure, its rich documentation, its representation of Eastern customs and mores, and its perceived moral value. Galland assessed the tales' value in this manner: "Provided those who will read those tales be disposed to benefit from the examples of virtue they will find there, they will be able to gain something which cannot be drawn from reading the other tales, which are more likely to corrupt morals than correct them."[23]

The success of *The Thousand and One Nights* exceeded all expectations. When the publisher judged that Galland was taking too long to submit succeeding volumes, she interfered, completing the eighth with two tales by another orientalist, François Pétis de La Croix. Scandalized by such lack of respect toward the original work, Galland moved the rest of his work to a different publisher, Florentin Delaulne.

Galland remained concerned that his source manuscript was incomplete. For the last four volumes, therefore, Galland took his inspiration from narratives that were relayed to him in Paris beginning in 1709 by a certain Hanna, a Maronite Christian from Aleppo. The significant changes and enrichments that Galland brought to those texts are the reasons for his exceptional fame. Two of the new tales, "Aladdin" and "Ali Baba," spread back to the East, where they were rapidly translated into Arabic. Similarly, it was also Galland's version of Shahriar and Scheherazade's frame narrative that established the canonical conclusion of *The Thousand and One Nights*, with its salvation for Scheherazade and redemption for Shahriar. Galland's *Thousand and One Nights* was imitated immediately, sometimes quite remarkably, as in *Les Mille et un jours* (The Thousand and One Days), a collection of Persian tales faithfully translated by François Pétis de La Croix,[24] or in *Les Mille et un quart d'heure* (The Thousand and One Quarters of an Hour), pseudo-Tartar tales by Thomas-Simon Gueullette.

Notes

1. In *Naissance de l'écrivain. Sociologie de la littérature à l'âge classique* (Paris: Editions de Minuit, 1985).

2. Galland, *Sommaire ou Mémoire chronologique*, 4.

3. Ibid., 5.

4. Wojciech Bobowski (1610–75), alias Albertus Bobovius or Haly-Beg, was kidnapped when he was about eighteen years old and later taken to Constantinople. There, introduced in the seraglio, this exceptional polyglot played a major role in diffusing Ottoman culture into the West. In particular, he authored the important "Relation du sérail du Grand Seigneur" ("Report from the Great Lord's Seraglio"), published in 1667.

5. Guillaume-Joseph Grelot (1630–?) is the author of a "Relation nouvelle d'un voyage de Constantinople, enrichie de plans levés par l'auteur sur les lieux & figures de tout ce qu'il y a de plus remarquable dans cette ville" ("New Report from a Journey to Constantinople, Enriched with Sketches Drawn by the Author of Places and Figures Representing What Is the Most Remarkable in That City"), published in 1680. Galland was in contact with him from 1672 through 1673.

6. Jean Chardin (1643–1713), French traveler and author of *Voyage en Perse et aux Indes orientales* (Travels to Persia and the Eastern Indies) in 1711.

7. Laurent d'Arvieux (1635–1702) was sent by Louis XIV with the letters that were demanded by the Great Vizir for renewing the Capitulations. He left behind the "Mémoires du chevalier d'Arvieux, envoyé extraordinaire du roi à La Porte, consul d'Alep, d'Alger, de Tripoli, & autres échelles du Levant, contenant ses voyages à Constantinople, dans l'Asie, la Syrie, la Palestine, l'Egypte et la Barbarie" ("Memoirs of the Chevalier d'Arvieux, Special Envoy to the King in La Porte, Consul of Aleppo, Algiers, Tripoli, and Other Ladders in the Levant, Including His Travels to Constantinople, to Asia, Syria, Palestine, Egypt, and Barbaria"), which were published in 1735.

8. Cornelio Magni (1638–1702) was the Italian scholars' correspondent. He wrote "Quante di piu curioso, e vago ha potuto racorre Cornelio Magni nel primo [e secundo] biennio de esso consumato in viaggi, e dimore per la Turquia" ("All the Many Curious and Beautiful Things Cornelio Magni Was Able to Gather in His first [and second] two-year trip to and around Turkey," 1679–92).

9. Thomas Smith (1638–1710) and Galland met during one of Galland's sojourns in Constantinople. In 1668–71, Smith was the chaplain of Sir Daniel Harvey, the British ambassador to Constantinople. He wrote many books, among which was "Septem Asiæ ecclesiarum notitia" ("Notice on the Seven Churches of Asia"), published in 1672.

10. John Covel (1638–1722) was the chaplain of the Levant Company. He lived in the East from 1670 to 1679 and wrote a journal during that time. That journal is still partially unpublished. However, in 1722 he published "Some Account of the present Greek Church."

11. Sir Paul Rycaut (1628–1700) was appointed consul to Smyrna by the Levant Company in 1667, and he stayed there for eleven years. He published "The History of the Present State of the Ottoman Empire" in 1701.

12. Pierre-Daniel Huet (1630–1721) was the bishop of Avranches, and he also authored a famous literary treatise entitled "De l'origine des romans" ("On

the Origin of the Novel"), published in 1669 as preface to *Zaïde*, Madame de Lafayette and Jean Regnault de Segrais's novel. That treaty is considered one of the first historical essays devoted to that literary genre.

13. Sir George Wheeler (1650–1723) was an English traveler, whose collection of antiquities was afterwards bequeathed to Oxford University.

14. Jacob Spon or Jacques Spon (Lyon 1647–Vevey, Switzerland, 25 December 1685), a French doctor and archaeologist, was a pioneer in the exploration of the monuments of Greece and a scholar of international reputation. He traveled to Italy, Greece, Constantinople, and the Levant from 1675 through 1676 in the company of Sir George Wheeler.

15. Thierry Bignon (1632–97) belonged to an illustrious family of bibliophilic jurists and scholars. He was also the son-in-law of Omer Talon, and as such, he had been trained in Port Royal before becoming the first president of the Great Council ("le Grand Conseil") in 1690.

16. This suffix refers to the works whose titles end as such: later *Ménagiana* and *Segraisiana*. In the present case, it is a collection of quotes and elegant (or pithy) phrases from different Eastern authors.

17. Bidpai (or Bidpay) is also known in French as Pilpay (see note 18).

18. Gilbert Gaulmin (1585–1665) published the "Livre des lumières ou La conduite des rois, composé par le sage Pilpay, indien, traduit en François par David Sahid d'Ispahan" ("The Book on the Enlightenment, or The Conduct of Kings, Composed by the Wise Pilpay, Indian, translated in French by David Sahid of Isfahan") (Paris: S. Piget, 1644).

19. Galland, *Lettre à Gisbert Cuper*, 8 September 1712.

20. Galland, *Avertissement, Mille et une nuit* (Paris: Barbin, 1704),1: ix–x.

21. Galland, *Lettre à Pierre-Daniel Huet*, 19 October 1701.

22. Galland's quote from the *Avertissement* preceding his *Mille et une nuit*, (Paris: Veuve Barbin, 1704), 1: viii.

23. Ibid., x.

24. See Paul Sebag's remarkable critical edition (Paris: Phébus, 2003) and the recent edition by editors Raymonde Robert, Pierre Brunel, Christelle Bahier-Porte, and Frédéric Mancier under the direction of Jean-François Perrin (Paris: Champion, 2010).

Antoine Galland's Works

Translations of Historical, Scientific, and Moral Works

La Mort du sultan Osman ou Le rétablissement de Mustapha sur le trône. Traduit d'un manuscrit turc de la Bibliothèque du roi. Paris: Barbin, 1678.

De l'Origine et du progrès du café. Sur un manuscrit arabe de la Bibliothèque du roi. Caen-Paris: Cavelier-Delaulne, 1699; 2nd ed. Paris: La bibliothèque, "L'écrivain voyageur," 1992.

Translations of Literary Works

Les Paroles remarquables, les bons mots, et les maximes des Orientaux. Traduction de leurs ouvrages en arabe, en persan et en turc, avec des remarques. Paris: Bénard-Brunet, 1694; 2nd ed. Abdelwahad Meddeb. Paris: Maisonneuve et Larose, 1999.

Les Mille et une nuit, contes arabes. Traduits en français par Mr Galland. Vols.1–8, Paris: Veuve Barbin, 1704–09; Vols9–12, Paris: Delaulne, 1712–17.

Les Fables indiennes, politiques et morales de Bidpaï Bramin ou philosophe indien, traduction de la langue turque [manuscript]. Paris: Bibliothèque Nationale de France, #6133; revised ed. Thomas-Simon Gueullette, 2 vols. Paris: Ribou, 1724.

Les Mille et une nuit. Ed. Jean-Paul Sermain and Aboubakr Charaibi. Paris: Flammarion, 2004.

Les Mille et une nuit. Ed. Manuel Couvreur. Paris: Champion, forthcoming 2011.

Works (Not Translations)

Journal (1708–1715) [manuscript]. Paris: Bibliothèque Nationale de France, #15279–80; partial ed. Henri Omont. In Mémoires de la Société de l'Histoire de Paris et de l'Île de France, XLVI (1919): 25–156.

Sommaire ou Mémoire chronologique de la vie d'Antoine Galland [manuscript]. Paris: Bibliothèque Nationale de France, #11403; ed. Henri Omont. In Mémoires de la Société de l'histoire de Paris et de l'Île de France, XLVI (1919): 5–14.

Histoire de l'esclavage d'un marchand de Cassis, à Tunis [manuscript]. Paris: Bibliothèque Nationale de France, #14963; eds. Catherine Guénot and Nadia Vasquez. Paris: La bibliothèque, "L'écrivain voyageur," 1993.

Smyrne ancienne et moderne [manuscript]. Bruxelles: Bibliothèque royale de Belgique, Mss II 5359; eds. Manuel Couvreur and Didier Viviers. Voyages inédits. Vol. 1. Paris: Champion, 2001.

Journal (1672–1673) [manuscript]. Paris: Bibliothèque Nationale de France, #6088–6089 (reprint); ed. Charles Schefer. Paris: Leroux, 1881. Frankfurt am Main: Institute for the history of Arabic-Islamic Science at the Johann Wolfgang Goethe University, 1994; Paris: Maisonneuve & Larose, 2002.

Voyage fait dans le Levant [manuscript]. cod. Gall. 727–28, 2 vols. Munich: Staatsbibliothek; eds. Manuel Couvreur and Didier Viviers. Voyages inédits. vol. 2. Paris: Champion, forthcoming 2011.

Correspondence

Antoine Galland, Correspondance. Ed. Mohamed Abdel-Halim, unpublished complement of dissertation. Imprimés (printed matters): 4–LN27–88230. Paris: Bibliothèque Nationale de France, 1964.

English Translations

Arabian Nights Entertainments. Trans. Bell. 2 vols. London: A. Bell, 1706.
The Arabian Nights (based on the text of the Fourteenth-Century Syrian manuscript edited by Muhsin Mahdi). Trans. Husain Haddawy. 2 vols. New York: Knopf (Everyman Library), 1992, 2007.

Secondary Literature

Abdel-Halim, Mohamed. *Antoine Galland: Sa vie et son œuvre.* Paris: Nizet, 1964.
Chraïbi, Aboubakr (dir.). *Les Mille et une nuits en partage.* Arles: Actes Sud, 2004.
———. Les Mille et une nuits. Histoire du texte et classification des contes. Paris: L'Harmattan, 2008.
Dufrenoy, Marie-Louise. *L'Orient romanesque en France (1704–1789.)* 3 vols. Montréal-Amsterdam: Beauchemin-Rodopi, 1946.
Irwin, Robert. *The Arabian Nights: A Companion.* London: Tauris, 1994; 2004.
Larzul, Sylvette. *Les Traductions françaises des Mille et une nuits. Étude des versions Galland, Trébutien et Mardrus.* Paris: L'Harmattan, 1996.
May, Georges. *Les Mille et une nuits d'Antoine Galland ou Le chef-d'œuvre invisible.* Paris: PUF, 1986.
Sermain, Jean-Paul. *Les Mille et une nuits entre Orient et Occident.* Paris: Desjonquères, 2009.

IV

Didacticism

Jeanne-Marie Leprince de Beaumont
Eighteenth-Century France

Jeanne-Marie Leprince (or Le Prince) de Beaumont

1711–1780?

Elisa Biancardi

(translated and adapted by Sophie Raynard)

Astonishingly modern, while at the same time faithful to an endur-
ing tradition, Jeanne-Marie Leprince de Beaumont's extraordinary work
and personality were long unappreciated. Biographical fictions, to whose
spread the author herself at times contributed, insured that readers were
rarely neutral. Recent and ongoing research allows corrections of some
traditional ideas about Jeanne-Marie Leprince de Beaumont, a more rigorous assessment of her life, and a more positive analysis of her work.
Earlier scholars focused primarily on Leprince de Beaumont's fairy tales
or on her pedagogical methods. Contemporary scholars who are exam-
ining the entirety of her varied corpus are claiming for her a profound
impact on the history of the periodical press, feminism, and the epistolary
novel, and even attributing to her a possible influence on the progressive
literature of the Enlightenment based on the critical attitude (similar
to the philosophers' dispute) that colored her pedagogical and Christian
passion vis-à-vis social inequalities of her time.

Marie-Barbe—who later changed her first name to Jeanne-Marie—
was born in Rouen on 26 April 1711. She was the eldest daughter of
the painter and sculptor Jean-Baptiste Nicolas Leprince and Marie-Barbe

Plantart,[1] After she lost her mother when she was eleven, she entered the convent of Ernemont, near Rouen, to be trained as a teacher. She later reported how she had heard "with ecstasy that two ladies of the first merit were at the head of an academy where they taught future school mistresses." She then continued: "No one could prevent me from flying there[, . . .] and I shared my inclination with one of my sisters. The two of us spent ten years in that academy."[2] In 1733, she also made the decision to begin her novitiate, but two years later, in 1735, she resolved to leave the convent.

Documents recently brought to light[3] suggest that the dozen years after that decision were a tormented period in her life. For a long time it was believed that she had married twice. The first marriage was supposed to have been a mismatch in which an exnovice serving as a governess and also as a lady's companion at the Lunéville Polish court married an officer, Antoine Grimard de Beaumont, in a union that ended after the birth of their daughter, Elisabeth, and an annulment in 1745 after two years of marriage. A second marriage, made possible by the annulment of the first one, was allegedly contracted in London around 1757, with a compatriot from Normandy, Thomas Pichon-Tyrrel. Recent discoveries raise doubt about the official nature of both relationships and leave some room for speculation about a situation that seems to have been considerably more complex.

A marriage celebration did, in fact, take place in Marie Leprince's life, but it was considerably earlier, in different circumstances, with a groom whose identity differed considerably from the version that Leprince herself later offered. Her first wedding was undertaken against her father's will on 25 June 1737. Her duties in Lunéville were not those of a governess but rather of "Musician of his Majesty the King of Poland," and her husband—far from being an "officer" named Grimard de Beaumont—was a certain Claude-Antoine Malter, who earned his living as master dancer. He probably belonged to that "dynasty of French dancers and pedagogues who perform[ed] in Europe in the eighteenth century," whose most famous representatives became known for their dissipation and their taste for places of debauchery.[4] Many details situate Marie-Jeanne Leprince de Beaumont in this unexpected milieu and confirm the famous autograph from the Morrison collection attributed to her. There the letter's author, deploring the "pagan" excesses of her youth, noted: "The unfortunate talent of a very beautiful voice was keeping me in the world, whose danger I knew; and the necessity of living from that talent obstructed all projects for reform [. . .]. If obedience to an enlightened director had not restrained my writing, I would have taken off the mask which covers me in the eye of the public; all I had to do was to take back my family name under which I scandalized so much, but then I would scandalize even more."[5]

It is not possible to ascertain the truth of suspicions about Madame Leprince de Beaumont's life. Nonetheless, that document, along with contemporary "revelations" long considered unimaginable for their detailed and explicit description of the author's presumed distractions, coincide with recently acquired data and confirm the identity and the profession of her first husband[6] as the master dancer Antoine Malter.

As for another of Marie Leprince's liaisons, the presence at her side of a partner named Beaumont[7] is very likely. She signed her first publications in 1748 with the initials "Le P. de B." or "Le Prince D. B.," but a legal matrimonial bond with Beaumont is difficult to imagine. A letter that Marie wrote much later to Thomas Pichon, when she envisaged marrying him, alludes clearly to the fact that, while having had excellent reasons to obtain an annulment of her first marriage to Malter (whom she refrained from naming), she avoided officially ratifying that annulment. As a result, while feeling free in her conscience, in the eyes of the law she was still married to Malter. So muddled a situation must have not only prevented her from marrying Beaumont—should she have wished to do so[8]—but must also have created difficulties for her when the time came, around 1757, to legalize her union with Pichon.

What we know for certain is that 1748 marked her literary debut with the publication of three books, one after the other, under the name Leprince de Beaumont. The first was *Le Triomphe de la vérité* (The Triumph of Truth), a short novel aiming at showing that natural understanding is sufficient for individuals to discover the existence of God; the second was the *Lettre en réponse à l'"Année merveilleuse"* (Letter in Response to the "Marvelous Year"), which was then followed by the *Arrêt solennel de la nature* (the Solemn Decrees of Nature), both polemic pamphlets in the traditional genre of the vindication of women.

Leprince de Beaumont's first three efforts, simple though they were, prefigured her later literary production. Having begun writing relatively late in life—at thirty-seven—she expressed her views firmly as products of mature experience. Certain ideas returned repeatedly: women's social rights, pedagogical advice based on experience, and the role of morals and faith. Yet for her, morals and faith had to be guided by reason in order to be individually achieved.

Given her personal morality, Leprince de Beaumont must have endured internal crises throughout her sentimental tribulations. Yet those personal crises never seemed to have diminished the sincerity of her adherence to Christianity. On the contrary, her works and her personal correspondence project a deep conviction that fueled her legendary moral energy. She must have relied heavily on the support of a strong piety in the face of the many concrete difficulties that assailed her morality.

In spite of a favorable public response to her works and the dedication of her first novel to the Polish king Stanislas in Lunéville, her initial three books did not draw the attention of the Lunéville court. Thus, at the end of 1748 she determined to leave the continent and try her luck in England. There she remained until 1763, her activity as an educator and woman of letters crowned with success. As a governess, she rapidly came to the attention of influential London families whose daughters or grand-daughters she educated, such as the Oglethorpes, John Carteret, Earl Granville, Lord Hillsborough, Frederick North 2nd Earl of Guilford, Charles Windham 2nd Earl of Egremont. Her pupils may well have inspired her famous *Magasins* (Magazines), the instructional manuals that she published. Madame Leprince de Beaumont's teaching duties led to solid friendships with people such as Sophia Carteret, soon to be the wife of William Earl of Shelbourne, and Lady Frances Mayne and her husband, the future Lord Newhaven and peer of Ireland. She also attended prestigious salons, such as Lady Montagu's, where she met Madame du Boccage[9] during her 1750 visit to London. Her professional and social success was reinforced and sustained by her continuing literary production: starting in 1750 she regularly "entertained" her readers of both sexes and all ages with epistolary fiction, encyclopedic popularizations, and pedagogical dialogues. The *Lettres diverses et critiques* (Various Letters and Critiques)—collections of often deliberately polemical writings on topics that were dear to her, such as the superiority of friendship over love, children's education, and the danger of improper books—were followed in the same year by *Le Nouveau Magasin français* (The New French Magazine), a monthly periodical on current cultural events, which she founded and directed for three years. That publication represented one of the first female contributions to francophone periodical press. Alongside different authors' literary works and scientific or technological popularizations, she herself contributed a large number of personal publications, including, in episodic installments, the *Lettres de Madame du Montier à [. . .] sa fille* (Letters from Madame du Montier to [. . .] Her Daughter), an epistolary novel whose style and content might have allowed some contemporaries to compare them with Marie de Rabutin-Chantal, Marquise de Sévigné's lettres (letters) or with Anne-Thérèse de Marguenat de Courcelles or Madame de Lambert's avis (advice) to her daughter.[10]

After her *Education complete* (Complete Education), a series of works specifically dedicated to teaching, Marie returned to the narrative genre in 1754. She set *Civan, roi de Bungo* (Civan, King of Bungo), a pedagogical novel, in sixteenth-century Japan. Dedicated to the then adolescent Joseph II of Austria, it proposed economic and social reforms that recall the enlightened and tolerant despotism of her contemporaries, the physiocrats. It is also possible to recognize the germ of reforms that Joseph II undertook when he came to the throne in 1765.[11]

In 1756 the *Magasin des enfants* (The Young Misses' Magazine), the most famous of her pedagogical manuals, was published. Soon translated into several languages, it was considered an essential didactic instrument for the next hundred years. Constantly reedited and updated, that book—whose fame also derived from the insertion of "La Belle et la Bête" ("Beauty and the Beast") and other fairy tales—definitively established the author's international celebrity.

Madame Leprince de Beaumont also thought it would be sensible to diversify the content of her dialogue-based manuals according to age, sex, social class, and the religious orientation of their addressees and was the first female educator to do so, writing a total of seven different *Magasins* (Magazines). The second manual, dedicated to female adolescents (1760), continued to be published in England, whereas the others, respectively, dedicated to young ladies, people from disadvantaged backgrounds, believers of all denominations, school-aged boys, and finally, devotees of the Catholic church, belonged to the last period of her life.

A key year in her professional life, 1756, also was memorable in her personal life. In that year, she fell deeply in love with her compatriot Thomas Pichon, a colonial official who had settled in London under the name Tyrrel, after having participated on the English side in the French-British conflict in Canada. He was a talented but enigmatic and conflicted bibliophile who did not hesitate to hide from her his treasonous acts toward France. He also tried, with less success, to do the same with his inveterate inclination for libertinage, and Jeanne-Marie's serene relationship with him soon fell into turmoil. After having been sealed by a more moral than legal commitment, their union was put into question in 1763, following the serious crisis[12] precipitated by Marie Leprince de Beaumont's return to the continent. Envisaged as a temporary distancing rather than as a definitive separation, her departure did in fact mark the end of the couple's relationship.[13] However, that situation—as attested by the "long philosophical dialogue"[14] of their ensuing correspondence—had the positive effect of settling their feelings and sublimating their passion, transforming it into a deep mutual attachment, more detached, sincere, and trusting than before.

On her return to France, Leprince de Beaumont first settled in Savoy, near Annecy. From 1773 onwards she lived in Avallon in Burgundy, still in the company of her daughter Elisabeth,[15] who in the meantime had married the surgeon Nicolas Louis Joseph Moreau. In France, Leprince de Beaumont continued to lead an intensely committed life, divided between her intellectual activities and new family responsibilities. Wishing to contribute to the Moreaus' well-being, she participated in the education of their numerous children, bought properties, and worked enthusiastically to help them prosper in terms of landholdings as well as of finance. In brief, she was often so busy that she could not find "the time to blow [her] nose."[16] The same dynamic spirit helped her overcome mental fatigue: during the course of those years, her epistolary exchange multiplied. She stayed in contact with Pichon and with her loyal friend Lady Mayne and responded, as expected, to the numerous admirers that her literary success had brought her. Among those were the Countess Kameke and the Prince Louis-Eugène of Wurtemberg, the ambassador of Sardinia, the Marquise de Choiseul-Meuse, Madame de Sauvigny, the Duchess of Villahermosa, and the Countess of Torre Palma, who was the Spanish ambassadress to France. Another prestigious proof of her celebrity is the "considerable present"—as Voltaire called it—that Empress Catherine of Russia gave her in 1767 in acknowledging the respect her court had shown for her works.[17] A mine of information both on the quantity and on the quality of the admirers whom Leprince de Beaumont attracted, her correspondence is crucial to understand her complex and still little-known persona. Her epistolary exchange with Thomas Pichon, emotionally moving because of its deep human and philosophical dialogue, also reveals the author's radically professional attitude and her very modern personal autonomy in her management of the publishing world's financial and advertising realities.

Madame Leprince de Beaumont's last works mixed educational manuals with narrative fictions. Her *Instructions pour les jeunes dames* (Instructions for Young Ladies; 1764) was followed by epistolary novels, published at the rate of one per year: *Lettres d'Emérance à Lucie* (Letters from Emérance to Lucie; 1765), *Mémoires de Madame la baronne de Batteville* (Memoirs of the Baroness de Batteville; 1766), and *La Nouvelle Clarice* (The New Clarissa; 1767). While less ambitious than *Civan*, *Clarice* still attempted to recapture her reformist inspiration. In 1767 she also published *Le Magasin des pauvres, artisans, domestiques et gens de la campagne* (Magazine for the Poor, Craftsmen, Domestics, and Country People), then in 1769 *Les Américaines* (American Women), a doctrinal manual leaning towards oecumenism. In 1772 and 1773 came the twelve volumes of the *Mentor moderne* (the Modern Mentor), a work specially conceived for the education of boys. After her *Contes moraux* (Moral Tales; 1773) and her *Nouveaux Contes moraux* (New Moral Tales; 1776), her last work was *La Dévotion éclairée ou Magasin des dévotes* (The Enlightened Devotion or the Magazine of Devout Women; 1779), a year before her presumed death.[18]

The didactic genre of the *Magazines* had made Leprince de Beaumont famous throughout Europe, and she completed the circle of her career as an author with a book that defined religious piety as "enlightened."[19] In this way, she emphasized one last time the same reconciliation between reason and faith, which thirty years or so earlier had inspired her *Triomphe de la vérité* (Triumph of Truth) and that had later constituted the optimistic foundation of her moral and cultural teachings.

Notes

1. Prosper Mérimée's future great-grandmother, she became in 1733 the half-sister of Jean-Baptiste Leprince, who was later celebrated as a painter.

2. *Education complète* (1752), "Avertissement," here (Lyon: Duplain, 1762), xxviii–xxix.

3. See correspondence.

4. Philippe Le Moal (dir.), *Dictionnaire de la danse*, "Malter" (Paris: Larousse, 1999); P. Estrée, *Artistes et Musiciens du XVIIIe siècle d'après des documents inédits*, "Le Menestrel," 1897.

5. Paul Bonnefon, *Autographes et documents*, "R.H.L.F." (346), vol. 13, 1906.

6. In particular, the police report dated November 1750, completed after 1 September 1751, and the letter from the Pastor Deschamps to Formey, dated 1764.

7. That presence was later confirmed in 1752 by the countersignature "A. Beaumont" in a publication contract with the publisher Nourse. That document was pointed out by Patricia Clancy to Geneviève Artigas-Menant (Artigas-Menant, 58).

8. This was a possibility that the letter (Vire 165 (B14) I, piece 5) seems to exclude.

9. In *Recueil des oeuvres de Madame du Boccage*, see the letter that she wrote to her sister on 25 May 1750 (Lyon: Frères Périsse, 1770), 3: 49.

10. Especially the "Lettre de M***" to the publisher and the latter's advice in the later Frankfurt and Leipzig edition (Knoch and Elsinger, 1757).

11. One striking correlation among others is Marie's strong questioning of monastic properties and contemplative orders and Joseph II's suppression of convents devoid of social utility.

12. To learn more about the reasons for that crisis and about the still unfruitful research on the wedding deed of the couple as well as Pichon's military spying activities, see Artigas-Menant, 63–65, 60–61, 324–25.

13. After many promises, hesitations, and dismissals, Pichon ended up aborting his project of joining her.

14. This is the way Artigas-Menant (58) defines their exchange, which was a medley of minute everyday details and vast intellectual or metaphysical speculations.

15. Or her "niece," as the author, in her correspondence, has always defined the young lady, apparently born from her legitimate marriage with Malter, but carrying the name Grimard. In any case, it was to follow Elisabeth that Marie moved to Burgundy in 1773 (according to Pichon's letter to Marie Leprince, dated 3 October 1773, photocopy from the Vire Public Library), when Nicolas Moreau, the young woman's husband, settled in Avallon to practice surgery.

16. Letter to Pichon, dated March 1767, Vire 165 (B14) I, piece 24.

17. See the letter dated 24 June 1767 (*Voltaire's Correspondence*, ed. Th. Besterman [Genève: Institut et Musée Voltaire, 1953], 66: 43.) A previous present from the same court had allowed the author to publish *Le Magasin des enfants* in 1756 (see "Avertissement," xxii) from the Lyon edition (Reguilliat, 1758).

18. 1780 is the most frequently indicated date for her death by biographers, but no official documentation proves it.

19. "Éclairée."

Jeanne-Marie Leprince de Beaumont's Works

Didactic Works

Education complète, ou Abrégé de l'histoire universelle [. . .]. 3 vols. London: J. Nourse, 1752–53.

Magasin des enfants, ou Dialogues entre une sage gouvernante et plusieurs de ses élèves [. . .]. 4 vols. London: J. Haberkorn, 1756. [The first published English translation dated 1759 and was republished fourteen times between 1760 and 1819—four of which were in America.]

Magasin des adolescentes [. . .]. 4 vols. London: J. Nourse, 1760.

Instructions pour les jeunes dames, qui entrent dans le monde, se marient [. . .]. 4 vols. Lyon and Paris: Desaint and Saillant, 1764.

Le Magasin des pauvres, artisans, domestiques et gens de la campagne. 2 vols. London: J. Nourse, 1767.

Les Américaines, ou La preuve de la religion chrétienne par les lumières naturelles.
6 vols. Annecy: C. M. Durand, 1769.
Le Mentor moderne, ou Instructions pour les garçons et pour ceux qui les élèvent.
12 vols. Paris: Cl. Hérissant, 1772–73.
La Dévotion éclairée ou Magasin des dévotes. Lyon: P. Bruyset Ponthus, 1779.

Novels, Narratives, and Tales

Le Triomphe de la vérité, ou Mémoires de Mr. de La Villette. 2 vols in 1. Nancy:
H. Thomas, 1748.
Lettres de Madame Du Montier à la marquise de *** sa fille [. . .]. In Le Nouveau
magasin français, February 1750–November 1752; 1st separate ed. 2 vols.
Lyon: P. Bruyset Ponthus, 1756.
Civan, roi de Bungo, histoire japonaise. 2 vols. Londres: J. Nourse, 1754; 2nd ed.
(A. Déguise). Geneva: Slatkine, 1998.
Lettres d'Émérance à Lucie. 2 vols. Lyon and Paris: P. Bruyset Ponthus and Ch.
Saillant, 1765.
Mémoires de Madame la baronne de Batteville, ou La veuve parfaite. Lyon: P. Bruyset
Ponthus, 1766.
La Nouvelle Clarice, histoire véritable. 2 vols. Paris: Desaint, 1767.
Contes moraux. 2 vols. Lyon and Paris: Saillant, 1773.
Nouveaux contes moraux. 2 vols. in 1. Lyon: P. Bruyset Ponthus, 1776.

Periodicals

Le Nouveau magasin français, ou Bibliothèque instructive et amusante. London: Fr.
Changuion, January 1750–December 1752.

Polemical Writings

Lettre en réponse à l'"Année merveilleuse." Nancy: H. Thomas, no given date
[1748].
Arrêt solennel de la nature [. . .]. n.p. [Paris]: 1748.
Lettres diverses, et critiques. 2 vols. in 1. Nancy: H. Thomas, 1750.

Modern Editions

Kaltz, Barbara, ed. *Jeanne Marie Le Prince de Beaumont, Contes et autres écrits.*
Oxford: Voltaire Foundation, 2000.
Madame de Villeneuve, *La Jeune Américaine et les contes marins ("La Belle et*
la Bête"); Les Belles Solitaires. Madame Leprince de Beaumont, *Magasin*
des enfants ("La Belle et la Bête"), ed. Elisa Biancardi. Paris: Champion,
2008.

English Translations

Magasin des Enfants: or, The Young Misses Magazine, Containing Dialogues between a Governess and Several Young Ladies of Quality Her Scholars [. . .]. 2 vols. in 1. Madame Leprince de Beaumont. London: B. Long and T. Pridden, 1759.

Tatar, Maria. *The Classic Fairy Tales: Texts, Criticism*. New York: Norton, 1999.

———. *The Annotated Classic Fairy Tales*. New York: Norton, 2002.

Zipes, Jack. *Beauty and the Beast and Other Classic French Fairy Tales*. New York: Penguin Group, [1987] 1989.

Correspondence

Lettres de Marie Le Prince de Beaumont à Thomas Pichon, fondateur de la Bibliothèque de Vire, "Au pays Virois," ed. P. Bagot. 1922–23, 49–63, 61–64, 85–89, 65–72, 123–28, 155–60, 177–89 [Fragmentary publication of Jeanne-Marie's correspondence with Thomas Pichon].

Lettre du pasteur Deschamps: Berlin, Deutsche Staatsbibliothek, Nachlass Formey, Lettres de Deschamps, f° 20 sq.

Secondary Literature

Artigas-Menant, Geneviève. *Lumières clandestines: Les papiers de Thomas Pichon*. Paris: Champion, 2001.

———. "Les Lumières de Marie Leprince de Beaumont: Nouvelles données biographiques." *Dix-huitième siècle* 36 (2004): 291–301.

Fiche de police de novembre 1750, complétée après le 1er septembre 1751: Bibliothèque Nationale, ms, f.fr.10783, f° 47.

Hearne, Betsy. *Beauty and the Beast: Visions and Revisions of an Old Tale*. Chicago: University of Chicago Press, 1989.

Robert, Raymonde. *Le Conte de fées littéraire en France de la fin du XVIIe à la fin du XVIIIe siècle*. Paris: Champion, [1982] 2002.

Traité et acte de mariage de Marie-Barbe Leprince et de Claude-Antoine Malter: Archives de Lunéville, A.C. 328, 11, année 1737; B.M.S., 1737–39, p. 82; Minutes notariales, étude Guibal, Maître Thiriet 1718–1765, 8 E 13, acte 183 du 22 juin 1737.Warner, Marina. *From the Beast to the Blonde: On Fairy Tales and Their Tellers*. London: Chatto and Windus, 1994.

V

Traditionalization

Naubert
Late Eighteenth-Century and
Early Nineteenth-Century Germany

The Grimms
Nineteenth-Century Germany

Bechstein
Nineteenth-Century Germany

The Legacy of the Eighteenth-Century and Nineteenth-Century German Female Storytellers

Shawn C. Jarvis

The late eighteenth century was a turbulent time in the history of German life and letters. As the Enlightenment gave way to the romantic movement and the Napoleonic wars ravaged Europe, literary tastes and social structures shifted. In this era literacy rates in the general population and especially among women increased, and demand for more entertainment literature, above all novels, rose. Hence it was a period that was auspicious for the entry of female authors into the literary marketplace. An explosion of books by women ensued—3,900 titles attributed to female writers appeared between 1700 and 1800.[1] Contemporary social and literary sensibilities suggested women were suited to writing lyric poetry, novels or tales, travelogues, and educational tracts. All the literary activities consigned to the "female" realm lent themselves well to the production of fairy tales.

Not until the codification of the Grimm genre was there a one-dimensional vision of the fairy-tale genre, its writers and collectors, its intended audience, its literary agenda, and its socializing impact. Before or contemporaneous with the Grimms' landmark *Kinder-und Hausmärchen* (*KHM*), German-speaking women produced a broad range of fairy-tale forms that filled the accepted literary landscape relegated to them.[2] They participated in the mediation and documentation of earlier traditions and authored collections of didactic educational primers disguised as fairy tales. By 1800, the family and romance novel had become the domain of female writers; by 1810, writers such as Sophie Albrecht, Julie Berger, Caroline Auguste Fischer, Therese Huber, Caroline de la Motte-Fouqué, Caroline Pichler, Dorothea Schlegel, Sophie Tieck-Bernhardi von Knorring, and Johanna Isabella von Wallenrodt (many the wives, lovers, sisters, or muses of romantic writers)[3] published reworkings of individual fairy tales and sagas that struck a compromise between the generic demands of the fairy tale and the narrative structure of the romance novel.[4]

Starting with Benedikte Naubert's *Neue Volksmährchen der Deutschen* in 1789, women also participated in the historical documentation of fairy tales from the ancient or Germanic past and became avid collectors of local tales and legends. Other women mediated foreign traditions with translations and compilations from the *Arabian Nights* or the French tales of the *conteuses*. By the 1840s, the Grimms' tales were beginning to assert their primacy as *the* fairy tale, and a cottage industry produced KHM knock-offs, with titles like Henriette Kühne-Harkort's "Snow White: Freely Adapted from the Grimms." Over the course of the eighteenth and nineteenth centuries, German women published no less and probably more than eight hundred fairy-tales titles, as individual stories and as collections[5] and thus far outnumbered male authors of fairy-tale books.

The recovery of German women's fairy tales has been slow, because the supremacy of the Grimms' model in the popular and scholarly imagination long displaced German women's fairy-tale authors. Feminist research has, however, uncovered a rich trove of women's tales.[6] Their writers range from real-life queens, such as Catherine the Great and Elisabeth of Romania, to early feminists like Bettine von Arnim, Fanny Lewald, Louise Dittmar, and Hedwig Dohm. They also include canonically received authors, such as Marie von Ebner-Eschenbach and Ricarda Huch, and highly prolific and beloved writers of children's literature, like Marie Timme, Amalie Schoppe, Elisabeth Ebeling, and Agnes Franz. Their tales reveal a dialogic interaction between female writers and their readers.

Many thematic concerns reverberate in the nineteenth-century tales and collections of German-speaking women, both royal and plebian, canonically received writers of "high" literature and those denigrated to the nether realms of "children's literature." These themes become most transparent when viewed through the prism of life's way stations, the trajectory from the cradle to the grave.[7] Children in women's tales are not typically hapless victims of voracious witches, but instead active shapers of their destinies. When they come of age and start the standard fairy-tale separation from home, males journey *out* to adventure, while females journey *in* to self-awareness. Males, unlike their Grimm counterparts, return after the adventure to hearth and home, while females gain not a husband or material goods, but intellectual and spiritual treasures. In tale after tale, the fairy-tale quest for a life partner refracts the fairy-tale happy ending of marriage, presenting the striving for that union as misguided or even failed and often depicting wedlock as a state of resignation and loss where the tension between affinities and responsibilities is woefully apparent. When the tales move into the territory after marriage and examine family life (an examination completely lacking in "traditional" tales), they often valorize the duties and responsibilities of parenthood and the abandonment of the magical for the mundane. A significant marker of women's tales is their multigenerational nature; even and especially in old age, wise elders serve as mentors and family historians who take young initiates under their tutelage or show them the error of their ways.

The clear voice of the female storytellers usually tells the experience of a girl on the brink of adulthood, the standard fairy-tale rite of passage. What is different in women's tales is the locale of the passage, the characters involved, and prospects and rewards after the successful rite. Generally commenced and completed in an exclusively female community devoid of magical helpers and fawning suitors, the passage is not a solitary journey; instead, the girl learns life skills from mature women (not Grimms' murderous matrons) and magical wise women who share their own experiences as a morality play. Many of the female role models in women's works are unmarried, childless mentors who reject the redemption motif through marriage and instead are content with their lot in life as financially and emotionally independent individuals. Their success is often the result of their achievement in a primary female occupation: spinning. A deforming task in the Grimms' tales, spinning creates the space where female truths and experience are passed on, and the protagonist spins her way to autonomy. Female characters reap not material, but intellectual and moral rewards, brought about in the process of actively engaging in their life stories.

A full understanding of the legacy of German women storytellers will require further research and a reevaluation of our critical and theoretical apparatus. It is telling that many writers facilitate the female's rite of passage not only by a wise woman, but also through reading. In one of Benedikte Naubert's stories, the eponymous heroine, Velleda, departs that tale perusing a small book of "foreign sagas." We will need to keep reading and exploring how these "foreign" tales of women constitute a tradition of their own that continues to resonate in contemporary women's fairy-tale revisionings, to enable a rite of passage for these tales alongside their other, more well-known siblings.

Notes

1. See Fronius.
2. Women's fairy tales were not limited to novels and didactic tales, but also include dramas and other formats.
3. See Gallas and Runge for a list of works. Thiel discusses Friederike Helene Unger's "Prinz Bimbam" (1802), Caroline Auguste Fischer's "Selim und Zoraïde" (1802), Sophie Tieck-Bernhardi's "Das Vögelchen" (1802), and Naubert's "Der kurze Mantel" (1789).
4. See Runge, 210.
5. For bibliographies of German women's fairy tales published in the eighteenth and nineteenth centuries, see the appendices to Jarvis, "Literary Legerdemain," and Thiel. The number of authors and books cannot be ascertained with complete certainty because of the limitations of bibliographical reference sources.
6. See especially Jarvis, *Das Reich der Wünsche* and Jarvis and Blackwell. For an excellent overview of feminist fairy-tale scholarship from 1970 to 2000, see Haase, 15–63.
7. For a detailed overview of these themes in German women's tales, see Jarvis's afterword to *The Queen's Mirror*.

Secondary Literature

Anthony, William. *The Narration of the Marvelous in the Late Eighteenth-Century German Märchen.* Diss. Johns Hopkins University, 1982, 1983.

Blackwell, Jeannine. "Fractured Fairy Tales: German Women Authors and the Grimm Tradition." *Germanic Review* 62 (1987): 162–74.

———, and Susanne Zantop, eds. *Bitter Healing: German Women Writers, 1700–1830, an Anthology.* Lincoln: University of Nebraska Press, 1990.

———. "German Fairy Tales, A User's Manual: Translations of Six Frames and Fragments by Romantic Women." *Marvels and Tales* 14.1 (2000): 99–121.

Fronius, Helen. "Der reiche Mann und die arme Frau: German Women Writers and the Eighteenth-Century Literary Marketplace." *German Life and Letters* 56.1 (2003): 1–19.

————. *Women and Literature in the Goethe Era (1770–1820): Determined Dilettantes.* Oxford: Clarendon Press; New York: Oxford University Press, 2007.

Gallas, Helga, and Anita Runge. *Romane und Erzählungen deutscher Schriftstellerinnen um 1800. Eine Bibliographie mit Standortnachweisen.* Stuttgart: Metzler, 1993.

Haase, Donald. "Feminist Fairy-Tale Scholarship: A Critical Survey and Bibliography." *Marvels and Tales* 14.1 (2000): 15–63.

Jarvis, Shawn C. "Literary *Legerdemain* and the *Märchen* Tradition of Nineteenth-Century German Women Writers." Diss. University of Minnesota, 1990.

————. "Trivial Pursuit? Women Deconstructing the Grimmian Model in the *Kaffeterkreis.*" In *The Reception of Grimms' Fairy Tales: Responses, Reactions, Revisions,* ed. Donald Haase. Detroit: Wayne State University Press, 1993. 102–27.

————. "Feminism and Fairy Tales." In *The Oxford Companion to Fairy Tales,* ed. Jack Zipes. Oxford: Oxford University Press, 2000. 155–59.

————, ed. *Das Reich der Wünsche. Die schönsten Märchen deutscher Dichterinnen.* Munich: C. H. Beck, 2012.

————, and Jeannine Blackwell, eds. and trans. *The Queen's Mirror: Fairy Tales by German Women, 1780–1900.* Lincoln: University of Nebraska Press, 2001.

Runge, Anita. *Literarische Praxis von Frauen um 1800: Briefroman, Autobiographie, Märchen.* Germanistische Texte und Studien 55. Hildesheim: Olms-Weidmann, 1997.

Seifert, Lewis C. "On Fairy Tales, Subversion, and Ambiguity: Feminist Approaches to Seventeenth-Century *Contes de fées.*" *Marvels and Tales* 14.1 (2000): 80–98.

Thiel, Anne. "Verhinderte Traditionen: Märchen deutscher Autorinnen vor den Brüdern Grimm." Diss. Georgetown University, 2001.

Benedikte Naubert

Shawn C. Jarvis

Christiana Benedikte Hebenstreit Naubert was born on 13 September 1752 in Leipzig, the sixth child of a well-situated, academic family. She enjoyed an extraordinarily broad education for a woman of her times: through the efforts of her older brothers and her own autodidactic endeavors, her studies ranged from classical languages, philosophy, and history, to her favorite subjects of mythology and medieval history, along with French, English, and Italian. Yet while she benefited from an education generally only accorded men in her times, she maintained the proper level of propriety for a woman, mastering such traditional female arts as piano and harp, as well as needlework. In 1797, she moved to Naumburg when she married Lorenz Wilhelm Holderrieder, a wealthy merchant, who died three years later. At her family's urging, she remarried at fifty, this time to Johann Georg Naubert, and in that time became the adoptive mother to her younger brother's orphaned son. Naubert returned with her husband in 1818 to Leipzig to seek medical treatment for her failing eyesight; she died in 1819 of pneumonia before the operation could be performed.

Until her marriages, financial considerations were probably a major motivating factor for her literary prodigiousness: after her father's death, Naubert's writing supported the family and helped finance her brother's university education. Her first novel, *Heerfort und Klärchen, etwas für empfindsame Seelen*, appeared anonymously in 1779, when the author was

---

*Many appeared in multiple editions. First editions are given, where ascertainable.

twenty-seven. Between 1785 and 1797, she produced at least one novel per year, often more. In her thirty-three years of literary production, she penned thirty-six historical novels[1], numerous family sagas, novellas, short stories, and fairy-tale collections and at least fourteen translations of contemporary English novels.[2] Even when already blind and almost deaf, the writer continued to dictate her works until her death in 1819.

Although Naubert jealously guarded her anonymity as an author, she cultivated connections to female writers and readers. She was in contact with a number of women authors through close correspondences (Louise Brachman) and literary dialogues (Charlotte von Ahlefeld). Numerous other important writers of the day, including Caroline Schlegel-Schelling, Bettine von Arnim, Caroline Pichler, and Therese Huber commented in various venues about their respect for Naubert's work; von Arnim even won her brother Achim over as an admirer.[3] Naubert published stories and fairy tales in female-oriented venues, especially the *Frauentaschenbücher*[4] (ladies' literary pocketbooks), and in her fairy-tale collections, she often specifically addressed her audience as "die *Leserin*," the female reader.

Her anonymity as a writer was both a blessing and a curse. Until mid-career on the literary scene, Naubert affected a male persona, partially out of female propriety and possibly out of publishing concerns. She listed herself on title pages of her novels as *der Verfasser* (the male writer), clearly in the hopes of gaining critical attention for her work. Contemporary critics believed the author was a man because nonsentimental, historical novels were common for male authors, but certainly not for women, who typically produced sentimental romance novels. Her obvious erudition in subjects uncommon for female writers and her knowledge of foreign languages also suggested a male author. At the same time, before copyright protections, purloining of her ideas was something against which she, an anomyn, could not defend: Naubert's works served as "inspiration" to every writer from Achim von Arnim to Walter Scott. Modern critics have suggested anonymity allowed her to experiment with generic conventions and explore the literary possibilities of various discursive modes.

During her lifetime, Naubert's works were extremely popular and esteemed. One indication of her status was her publisher, Johann Friedrich Weygand; Wieland, Herder, and Goethe all were represented in his list of authors. The number of editions, reprints, and inclusions in anthologies and translations are also indications. Individual fairy tales from the *Neue Volkmährchen der Deutschen* (New German Folktales, 4 volumes, 1789–93) were often reprinted individually; they were also selected for inclusion in numerous anthologies of the best contemporary writers, such as *Sammlung der interessantesten Meisterwerke deutscher Dichter und Prosaisten* (Collection of the Most Interesting Masterpieces of German Writers), *Cabinets-Bibliothek der Deutschen Classiker* (Library of German Classics), and *Meyer's Groschen-Bibliothek der Deutschen Classiker* (Meyer's Penny Library of German Classics). Naubert was also a popular author for contemporary translators: at least six of her historical novels appeared in English and French, two in Dutch, one in Swedish, and one in Spanish.[5] Three fairy tales from the *Neue Volksmährchen der Deutschen* were translated into English, and an adaptation of one of her historical novels was acted on the London stage in 1795.

Naubert's fairy-tale œuvre covers a twenty-year period. Like her historical novels, her fairy tales showed great breadth and depth of knowledge of various traditions, gleaned from her extensive reading of medieval chronicles, legends, and sagas. Her first collection, *Neue Volksmährchen der Deutschen*, answered Johann Gottfried Herder's patriotic call to resurrect the Germanic past and establish connections to English tale-telling. Her fairy tales in this collection include her own interpretation of the Nibelungs and Tannhäuser sagas, the Arthurian tradition, her variants of Rübezahl and the Pied Piper of Hamelin, stories about Frau Holle, the Weiße Frau, and legends of Saints Ottilie and Genoveva. "Erlkönigs Tochter" ("The Erl-King's Daughter") and "Der kurze Mantel" ("The Short Cloak") harked back to ballads and songs Herder had recorded, and although the plan was never realized, Jacob Grimm had hoped to include "Ottilie" in a German legend collection.

Naubert's other fairy-tale collections presented non-Germanic material. *Alme, oder Egyptische Mährchen* (*Almé, or Egyptian Fairy Tales*, 5 volumes, 1793–97) treated the self-confident Alme and presented Naubert's own concept of Egypt.[6] *Heitere Träume in kleinen Erzählungen* (*Delightful Dreams in Short Tales*, 1806) presented "Fanchon vielleuse," "Persin-Persinet," and "Blanca Bella," her unique versions of tales by the *conteuses*.

Hallmarks of Naubert's fairy tales are the celebration of the female narrative voice and the focus on female experience. Recurring themes in her works are women's communities outside traditional society; the teaching of skills for intellectual and material independence; the interactions within female triads of magical wise woman, biological mother, and daughter; and most important, the mediation of the female's rite of passage by a wise woman, but also through reading.

Naubert's critical reception has varied over time. Her contemporaries initially praised her, then criticized her for not following Johann Karl August Musäus's model. The German romantics embraced and often emulated her work; scholars have traced her influence on writers from Walter Scott to Thomas Mann. Naubert has also become an important focus for recent feminist research: that scholarship has led to the recovery of other women (Friederike Helene Unger, Sophie Albrecht, Therese Huber, Caroline de la Motte-Fouqué, Dorothea Schlegel, and Sophie Tieck-Bernhardi von Knorring) who published individual fairy tales and saga reworkings before 1810. Feminist research has also shown how Naubert influenced and informed her female successors. Her works are enjoying renewed interest; her four-volume *Neue Volksmährchen der Deutschen* has recently been reissued, with critical commentary, in German and Spanish.

Notes

1. Of the 128 historical novels that appeared in Germany between 1780 and 1800, twenty-six (20 percent) were Naubert's and she was the only female writer. By her death in 1819, she had authored a total of thirty-six, covering almost every century from the fifth to the eighteenth and historical events such as the Crusades, the War of the Roses, the Thirty-Years' War, among others. See Henn, 545–46.

2. See appendix 1 in Hilary Brown.

3. See Brown, 15–18.

4. Naubert contributed to such illustrious journals as *Journal für deutsche Frauen*, *Selene*, *Frauenzimmer-Almanach zum Nutzen und Vergnügen*, *Minerva*, and *Die Harfe*.

5. A new reprint of *Neue Volksmährchen der Deutschen* in Spanish may shed more light on other translations of Naubert's works. See Benedikte Naubert and Genoveva Dieterich, *Cuentos populares alemanes* (Madrid: Ediciones Siruela, 2003). Other translations of her works most probably exist, but currently no comprehensive list is available.

6. See Oerke.

Benedikte Naubert's Works (by genre)

Fairy Tales, Folk Tales, and Magic Tales

Amalgunde Königin von Italien oder das Märchen von der Wunderquelle. Eine Sage aus den Zeiten Theoderichs des Großen (Amalgunde, Queen of Italy or the Fairytale of the Miraculous Spring: A Saga from the Times of Theoderic the Great). Leipzig: Weygand, 1787.

Neue Volksmährchen der Deutschen (New German Folktales). 4 vols. Leipzig: Weygand, 1789–92.
Alme oder Egyptische Mährchen (Alme, or Egyptian Fairytales). Leipzig: Beygang, 1793.
Velleda: Ein Zauberroman (Velleda: A Magical Novel). Leipzig: Schäfer, 1795.
Heitere Träume in kleinen Erzählungen (Delightful Dreams in Short Tales). Leipzig: [Weygand?], 1806.

Historical and Family Novels (a Selection)

Heerfort und Klärchen. Etwas für empfindsame Seelen (Heerfort and Clara: Something for Sensitive Souls). Frankfurt und Leipzig: Reiffenstein, 1779.
Geschichte Emma's, Tochter Kayser Karls des Grossen und seines Geheimschreibers Eginhard (The Story of Emma, Daughter of Charlemagne and His Secret Secretary Eginhard). Leipzig: Weygand, 1785.
Walter von Montbarry, Großmeister des Tempelordens. (Walter de Monbary, Grandmaster of the Knights Templar). Leipzig: Weygand, 1786.
Geschichte der Gräfin Thekla von Thurn oder Scenen aus dem dreyssigjährigen Kriege (History of Countess Thekla von Thurn or Scenes from the Thirty-Years' War). Leipzig: Weygand, 1788.
Elisabeth, Erbin von Toggenburg, oder Geschichte der Frauen von Sargans in der Schweiz. (Elisabeth, Heiress of Toggenburg, or the Story of the Women of Sargans in Switzerland). 2 vols. Leipzig: Weygand, 1789.
Herrmann von Unna. Eine Geschichte aus den Zeiten der Vehmgerichte (Hermann of Unna: A Story from the Times of the Secret Tribunals). Leipzig: Weygand, 1789.
Barbara Blomberg, vorgebliche Maitresse Kaiser Karls des Fünften. Eine Originalgeschichte in zwei Theilen. (Barbara Blomberg, Alleged Mistress of Kaiser Karl the Fifth: An Original Story in Two Parts). Leipzig: Weygand, 1790.
Alf von Dülmen: Oder Geschichte Kaiser Philipps und seiner Töchter; Aus den ersten Zeiten der heimlichen Gerichte (Alf von Dülmen, or the History of Emperor Philipp and his Daughters: From the Early Days of the Secret Tribunals). Leipzig: Weygand, 1791.
Eudocia, Gemahlinn Theodosius des Zweyten: Eine Geschichte des fünften Jahrhunderts (Eudocia, Wife of Theodosius the Second: A Story from the Fifth Century). Leipzig: Heinrich Gräff, 1805.
Rosalba. Leipzig: J. C. Hinrichs, 1818.

Novels Available in Translation during Naubert's Time*

ALF VON DÜLMEN

Alf von Deulmen; or, The History of the Emperor Philip, and his Daughters. Trans. A. E. Booth. London: Bell, 1794.

Les aveux d'un prisonnier, ou anecdotes de la cour de Philippe de Souabes. Trans. Jeanne Eléonore de Cérenville. Paris: Le Normant, 1803.

Adolphe de Dulmen. Paris: Le Normant, 1804.

ELISABETH ERBIN VON TOGGENBURG

Elisabeth, héritière du Tockenbourg, ou histoire des dames de Sargans. Paris: Dufart, 1792.

Feudal Tyrants; or, The Counts of Carlsheim and Sargans. A Romance. Taken from the German. Trans. Matthew Gregory [pseudo M. G. Lewis]. London: Hughes, 1806.

HEERFORT UND KLÄRCHEN

Heerfort en Klaartje of de zegepraal, der deugdzaame en standvaste liefde. Te Amsteldam: W. Wynands, 1787.

Heerfort and Clara. From the German. Trans. John Poulin. London: G. G. J. and J. Robinson, 1789.

Heerfort et Claire: Histoire allemande. London: Maradan, 1789.

HERMANN VON UNNA

Herman d'Unna, ou, Aventures arrivées au commencement du quinzième siècle, dans le temps ou le Tribunal secret avoit sa plus grande influence. Trans. Jean Nicolas Étienne de Bock. Metz: C. Lamort, 1791.

Herman of Unna: a Series of adventures of the fifteenth century, in which the proceedings of the secret tribunal under the emperors Winceslaus and Sigismond, are delineated. London and Dublin: G.G. and J. Robinson, 1794.

Herman de Unna: Rasgo historial de alemania. Trans. Bernardo Maria de Calzada. Madrid: Real, 1807.

ROSALBA

Rosalba, eller Uppwaknandet i Benediktinerkyrkan. Utur en i fält stupad officers papper. Öfwersättning från tyskan. Stockholm and Uppsala: Em Bruzelius, 1819.

THEKLA VON THURN

Thecla de Thurn, ou scènes de la guerre de 30 ans. Trans. Jeanne Eléanore der Cérenville. Paris: Pillet, 1815.

WALTER VON MONTBARRY

Walter de Monbary, grand-maître des templiers. Roman historique. Trans. Jeanne Eléanore de Cérenville. Paris: Maradan, 1797.
Het Leven van Walter van Montbarry, grootmeester van de Orde der Templeieren. In den Haage: J. C. Leeuwestijn, 1802.
Walter de Monbary, Grand Master of the Knights Templars: A Historical Romance. London: Lane and Newman, 1803.

Secondary Literature

Anthony, William. *The Narration of the Marvelous in the Late Eighteenth-Century German Märchen.* Diss. The Johns Hopkins University, 1982, 1983.
Blackwell, Jeannine. "Die verlorene Lehre der Benedikte Naubert: Die Verbindung zwischen Phantasie und Geschichtsschreibung." *Untersuchungen zum Roman von Frauen um 1800.* Ed. Helga Gallas and Magdalene Heuser. Tübingen: Niemeyer, 1990. 148–59.
———, and Susanne Zantop. *Bitter Healing: German Women Writers, 1700–1830, an Anthology.* Lincoln: University of Nebraska Press, 1990.
Brown, Hilary. *Benedikte Naubert, 1756–1819, and Her Relations to English Culture.* Bithell Series of Dissertations, vol. 27. Leeds: Maney Publishing for the Modern Humanities Research Association and the Institute of Germanic Studies, University of London, 2005.
Henn, Marianne, "Historiographie und Märchenfiktion: Benedikte Nauberts *Neue Volksmärchen der Deutschen.*" *Seminar: A Journal of Germanic Studies* 43.4 (2008): 545–53.
Jarvis, Shawn C. "The Vanished Woman of Great Influence: Benedikte Naubert's Legacy and German Women's Fairy Tales." In *In the Shadow of Olympus: German Women Writers from 1790–1810,* ed. Katherine R. Goodman and Edith Waldstein. Albany: State University of New York Press, 1991. 189–209.
———, ed. *Das Reich der Wünsche: Die schönsten Märchen deutscher Dichterinnen.* Munich: C.H. Beck, 2012.
———, and Jeannine Blackwell, eds. and trans. *The Queen's Mirror: Fairy Tales by German Women, 1780–1900.* Lincoln: University of Nebraska Press, 2001.
Krimmer, Elisabeth. "Neue Volksmärchen der Deutschen (Book)." *Seminar—A Journal of Germanic Studies* 39.3 (September 2003): 261–62.
Martin, Laura. "The Rübezahl Legend in Benedikte Naubert and Johann Karl August Musäus." *Marvels and Tales* 17.2 (2003): 197–211.
———. *Benedikte Nauberts* Neue Volksmärchen der Deutschen: *Strukturen des Wandels.* Würzburg: Königshausen und Neumann, 2006.

Naubert, Benedikte, Marianne Henn, Paola Mayer, and Anita Runge. *Neue Volksmärchen der Deutschen*. Göttingen: Wallstein, 2001.

Oerke, Catharina. *Gattungsexperiment und Ägyptenkonstruktion: Benedikte Nauberts "Alme oder Egyptische Mährchen" (1793–97)*. Göttingen: Göttingen Universitäts-Verlag, 2006.

Runge, Anita. *Literarische Praxis von Frauen um 1800: Briefroman, Autobiographie, Märchen*. Germanistische Texte und Studien 55. Hildesheim: Olms-Weidmann, 1997.

Sweet, Denis. "Benedikte Naubert." In Blackwell and Zantop, 201–06.

Thiel, Anne. *Verhinderte Traditionen: Märchen deutscher Autorinnen vor den Brüdern Grimm*. Thesis (Ph.D.) Georgetown University 2001.

———. "From Woman to Woman: Benedikte Naubert's 'Der kurze Mantel.'" In *Harmony in Discord*, ed. Laura Martin. Bern: Lang, 2001. 125–44.

Jacob Grimm

1785–1863

Wilhelm Grimm

1786–1859

Donald R. Hettinga

Wilhelm Grimm was, perhaps, more accurate than he could have imagined when he wrote in 1812 that it was "probably just the right time to collect these tales."[1] He believed that oral tradition was waning, but he also believed that the *times* were right for readers to embrace a collection that mixed entertainment with scholarship. Tentative at first, as the *Kinder-und Hausmärchen* (Children's and Household Tales) evolved through a decades-long series of editing to assume a literary form that met public taste, the embrace has become increasingly enthusiastic until at the present day, the fairy tales of the Brothers Grimm have become a totem of Western cultural identity. Although scholars have pointed out the literary character of the *Märchen* (tales) for decades, they still are widely believed to be transcriptions of an oral peasant tradition. In actuality, the sources of the tales, like the lives of the two brothers, are located somewhere between common and aristocratic classes and are an integral part of the early nineteenth century.

Born in Hanau, near Frankfurt am Main, roughly a year apart[2] and living and working together for their entire lives, the two brothers, Jacob Ludwig Carl Grimm and Wilhelm Carl Grimm, are popularly known as one entity—the Brothers Grimm. From early youth on, they spent most of their time together. They followed parallel paths through lyceum, university, and professional careers as scholars and librarians. They collaborated on numerous scholarly projects from the collection of fairy tales to the development of *Das Deutsche Wörterbuch*, a multivolume dictionary that describes German usage from Luther to the present. Jacob generally pursued linguistic and philological projects like his groundbreaking *Deutsche Grammatik* (German Grammar, 1819–31) and his *Geschichte der deutschen Sprache* (History of the German Language, 1848). Wilhelm preferred literary endeavors, essentially taking over the fifty-year project of collecting and editing the tales and publishing numerous editions of early Germanic poems. The brothers maintained close communication about everything they did. Domestically, even after Wilhelm married and had children, Jacob remained a part of his household. Only death separated the brothers.

To some extent, Jacob and Wilhelm's closeness grew out of their birth order as the two oldest surviving sons of the nine children born to Philipp Wilhelm Grimm and Dorothea Zimmer Grimm. Three of those siblings would live less than eighteen months, but it was the death of their father just days after Jacob turned eleven that brought profound change to the Grimms and placed Jacob and Wilhelm in a position that significantly contributed to their closeness. Because Philipp Grimm served as magistrate in the small town of Steinau from 1791 to 1796, the boys' early childhood was comfortable and protected.

The family's privileged life, complete with coachman and servants, was lost at Philipp's death in 1796. The family was immediately forced to move into a smaller, rented house. The world might not have heard anything more from the Brothers Grimm, if not for an aunt, Henriette Zimmer, lady-in-waiting to the *Landgräfin* (Countess) of Hesse, who sponsored Jacob and Wilhelm at the Cassel lyceum. In Cassel, the brothers lived on the margins of aristocratic society, taking classes along with courtiers and pages but rooming with the palace cook. Somewhat behind the other students in their preparation, the Grimms initially had to spend much of their time catching up. Often reminded of their lower social status, the brothers developed a strong fraternal bond and a lifelong sensitivity to social injustice.

As a magistrate's children, the Grimms did not initially qualify to attend university, but Jacob's appeal to Wilhelm I, *Landgraf* (Count) of Hesse-Cassel, to enroll at the University of Marburg was granted in 1802. Wilhelm, held back in part by age and in part by sickness, won his appeal the following year and, with some eagerness after having spent six months confined to his room because of asthma, moved to Marburg to join Jacob in the study of law, their father's profession and the vocation that their mother desired for them. While the brothers were more social than they had been in Cassel, both approached the academic regime in Marburg with earnestness. Although they dressed the part of student, at times sporting scarlet frock coats, leather pants, tall boots, and even spurs, the brothers eschewed the gambling and beer parties common to university life, choosing instead to attend salon-like entertainments where students and professors discussed books, danced, and performed bits of Shakespeare and other plays.

Jacob found himself bored or impatient with many of his professors, but Friedrick Karl von Savigny, a young expert in Roman law, engaged his attention. Savigny took the Grimms under his wing and was to be influential in shaping their future careers. Intellectually, Savigny pointed them in the direction of German culture and letters, arguing that Germanic history and ideas were as deserving of scholarly attention as the classical elements of the university curriculum. Socially, Savigny introduced them to his circle of romantic artists and friends. This linked them to Clemens Brentano and Achim von Arnim, Marburg literati with a passion for Germanic literature and significant financial means and social connections. Both would later play significant roles in the publication of the Grimms' tales.

In 1805 Jacob left Marburg to work for ten months as Savigny's research assistant in Paris. Paris not only broadened Jacob's cultural experience; it also developed skills in archival research and textual studies, matters central to his later professional life. But if the excursion to Paris was professionally rewarding, it was also very lonely for both brothers. They corresponded faithfully, offering each other advice and reaffirming their closeness.

After a brief reunion in Marburg, the brothers set up housekeeping in Cassel with the rest of their family. Instead of taking university examinations, Jacob sought work to provide for the household. Although unsuccessful in securing a librarianship at court, he did find a clerical position in the Hessian War Office. The work was drudgery, and Jacob

resented the accoutrements of court—the requisite uniform and pow-
dered wig—but the small income helped. The family relied on Jacob's
income for approximately a year until 1 November 1806, when Napoleon's forces entered Cassel, and French officials took over the government, renaming Hesse Westphalia with Jérôme Napoléon, the youngest
brother of the emperor, as king.

Both brothers were unemployed in 1807, a very lean year for the
family. There was income from the occasional sale of a literary essay, but
their main support came from packages of food and small gifts of money
sent from their aunt, Henriette Zimmer. Their circumstances became
even darker when, in May 1808, Dorothea Grimm became sick and died.

Their fortunes changed in July 1808. A friend spoke to Jérôme on
Jacob's behalf, opening the door to the librarianship he had previously
sought. Once again Jacob had to don a dress uniform on state occasions,
but his salary was ten times what it had been in the War Office, and
he enjoyed considerable freedom to pursue his own interests. Not much
of a bibliophile, Jérôme's one request of his new librarian was that he
write the words "Bibliothèque particulière du Roi" in large characters
over the door of the library.[3] The lack of official duties released Jacob
to work with Wilhelm collecting authentic German tales and legends.

The collection that would make their name famous throughout the
world began as collaboration with their friends Brentano and Arnim.
In 1805, Arnim and Brentano had published the first volume of *Des
Knaben Wunderhorn* (The Boy's Magic Horn), a collection of folksongs
that included a call for tales as they still were being told by ordinary
people. The brothers contributed a number of folksongs and, indeed,
played a significant role in the two subsequent volumes of Brentano and
Arnim's publication, with their younger brother Ludwig contributing a
frontispiece to the final volume. At the same time, Jacob and Wilhelm
began working on their own collection of tales, becoming more excited
by its potential after Philip Otto Runge, an artist, contacted Arnim
asserting that anyone who attempted a collection would find it worth-
while and rewarding. Runge furnished two tales, "The Juniper Tree" and
"The Fisherman and His Wife," stories that he claimed to have taken
down word for word from fishermen but that reflect considerable artistic
formulation. These stories would become among the best-known tales
in the *Kinder-und Hausmärchen*.

Perhaps the most pervasive misconception about the *Kinder-und
Hausmärchen* is that they were collected directly from peasants. Such
a notion has persisted because of its appeal to nineteenth- and twentieth-century readers, particularly those interested in German identity or

romantic literary principles. Wilhelm helped foster this misperception with language he used in his introductions to various volumes and editions of the collection. The tales, he says, "are part of a regular Sunday pastime in many places";[4] they have been preserved by the metaphorical hedges of the kitchen hearth, the attic stairs, the meadows and the forests, and "above all the untrammeled imagination."[5] The one source that Wilhelm acknowledged by name in the introductions was Dorothea Viehmann, whom, in the first edition, he characterized as a peasant woman from the village of Zwehrn near Kassel.

As scholars in recent decades have looked more carefully at the tales' sources, Wilhelm's characterization of the tales as folk products has generated considerable critical debate.[6] Revisionists have argued that Viehmann is more French than German, more middle class than peasant, with Alan Dundes and John Ellis accusing the Grimms of deception or fraud. To complicate this, another significant source, "Marie," identified by Wilhelm's son Herman as Marie Clare, an elderly servant, has been reidentified by Heinz Rölleke as far more likely to have been Marie Hassenpflug, the well-educated, teenaged daughter of an upper-middle-class Huguenot family.[7] Such revelations necessarily raise questions about the Grimms' methodology and the connection of the tales to an oral tradition.

The connection between the Grimms and the German folk is a qualified one. Jacob and Wilhelm did not eavesdrop outside thatched-roofed cottages as depicted in the 1962 Cinerama film *The Wonderful World of the Brothers Grimm*. However, they *did* interview some ordinary folk, such as an elderly soldier who swapped several stories for the Grimms' cast-off clothing. But the habits of two middle-class scholarly gentlemen did not put them in the paths of oral storytellers, and their attempts at field collection were mixed: because she had been put off by Brentano's disorganized recording methods in an earlier visit, one woman refused to tell Wilhelm any stories, although she agreed to let him record her narration when he brought his children along. Most of the collection came from middle-class or aristocratic friends who shared the Grimms' interest in Germany's cultural heritage and who gathered in coffee circles to tell stories that they had collected from servants, carters, and country folk or that they had encountered in their reading.

Jacob and Wilhelm also drew heavily on old manuscripts and texts, fastidiously comparing the tales they found with variants from other cultures. They believed the tales were "Naturpoesie," natural poetry that evolved from a pure folk source and that provided them with a paradigm insuring cultural integrity while allowing attention to literary shape.[8] Accurate transcription was crucial, but not simply to record an individual performance of a tale. The brothers recognized that tellers alter their tellings to fit rhetorical situations; as scholarly "tellers," they believed they had similar latitude to combine variants or to enhance a narrative to get at what they considered its essential form. Thus, in the preface to volume 2 of the first edition, Wilhelm wrote that "the aim of our collection was not just to serve the cause of the history of poetry: It was our intention that the poetry living in it be effective."[9] They would hold that editing for effectiveness was not the same as embellishing.

Wilhelm believed that their combinations and additions brought the tales closer to an ideal Germanic tale. He applied that criterion repeatedly throughout the more than two hundred pages of notes on the tales, comparing tales, whether from Serbia, India, or the plains Indians of North America with Germanic tales and motifs from older literature like the *Nibelungenlied* (Song of the Nibelungs). Even so, the Grimms had "a remarkable feel for the nature of folk literature" and "collected as much of the oral narrative tradition and documented it as 'faithfully' and as comprehensively as was possible for them under the existing conditions."[10]

Their work on the tales and other scholarly projects was to some extent a welcome distraction from pressing personal problems. Jacob discovered that working for Jérôme was not always as pleasant as he at first thought it might be. The requirement to converse in French in all official situations grated on both brothers. French secret police seemed to be everywhere in Cassel, and high taxes and an inflated cost of living quickly ate up Jacob's salary. Furthermore, Jérôme could be fickle: he once took over the library and gave Jacob only thirty-six hours to transfer twelve thousand volumes to the attic of another palace. That order nearly brought tragedy to the Grimms when that palace and many of Cassel's surrounding houses and buildings caught fire in November 1811, and Jacob risked his life rescuing valuable volumes.

Wilhelm struggled with chronic illness. Cardiac problems sent him to Halle where he endured the latest medical treatments, including complicated regimens of pills and powders, applications of mercury ointment, baths and alcohol washes, and electromagnetic therapy. But Halle's relative closeness to Berlin brought him visitors such as Brentano and Arnim, who coaxed him into visiting Berlin. Wilhelm's encounter with artists and literati there enlarged his view of the world and broadened his professional correspondence just as Jacob's earlier visit to Paris had expanded his. He summoned the courage to contact the revered author Goethe and initiated a correspondence with scholars and writers throughout Europe. His Halle sojourn also put Wilhelm in contact with the Haxthausen family who eventually provided the Grimms with twenty additional tales.[11]

Working on several projects simultaneously, as they typically did, both Grimms published their first books in 1811. Jacob's *Über den altdeutschen Meistergesang* (On Old German Mastersong) argued that medieval master songs used language that was artistically similar to that of the *Minnesang* (Courtly Love Poetry). Wilhelm's *Altdänische Heldenslieder, Balladen und Märchen* (Old Danish Heroic Songs, Ballads, and Tales) was a translation from Danish. Both were thematically related to the tale project, and both marked the beginning of the Grimms' attempt to present a canon of medieval German literature and to link that tradition to their own times.

Christmas 1812 saw the release of the *Kinder- und Hausmärchen*. Arnim had helped to convince Georg Reimer in Berlin to publish the tales. Despite rough economic times, the first volume sold fairly well. Without advertising, Reimer moved about three hundred copies per year, exhausting the initial print run of nine hundred in just three years. Rendered confident by this, Reimer agreed to publish a second volume.[12] Like the First Volume, it was not illustrated, but unlike the first, it didn't sell well. In the first four years after its appearance in 1815, Reimer sold only five hundred copies.[13]

During the politically turbulent middle teens of the century, the brothers continued to work with a broad body of folk literature. Between 1813 and 1816, they published three volumes of the journal *Altdeutsche Wälder* (Old German Forests); between them, the Grimms contributed some forty articles on topics ranging from Norse heroic poetry and Germanic legends to folk literature from Holland, France, Serbia, India, and other countries. In 1813, however, King Jérôme once again put demands on Jacob's time. As Napoleon's empire crumbled, he decided to carry off as many German cultural treasures as possible, and he ordered Jacob to ready books and artifacts for shipment to France. Through subversive selections, Jacob managed to save many of the best manuscripts, particularly those with a Hessian connection.

The brothers' actions during the period of Napoleonic hegemony demonstrate a reality that would surface several times during their lives—as strong as their love was for things German, and later, for a united Germany, Hesse was their first love. After the Russian liberation of Cassel in 1813, the Grimms' sense of patriotism was quickened.

Their younger brothers Carl and Ludwig volunteered for the army, and, poor though they were, Jacob and Wilhelm donated the proceeds from their 1815 publication, *Der Arme Heinrich* by Hartmann von Aue (Poor Henry), to rebuilding and protecting Hesse.

Editing the second volume of the *Kinder-und Hausmärchen* fell largely to Wilhelm, because Jacob, appointed secretary to the Hessian legation, traveled west with the army of liberation as it engaged Napoleon's forces. Despite the horrors and the hardships of war, Jacob searched libraries on the way, thrilled when he found rare manuscripts, such as a parchment copy of *Titurel* in Karlsruhe.[14] Upon the legation's arrival in Paris after Napoleon's abdication, Jacob was assigned the task of recovering books and objects plundered by the French.

That the second volume of the tales appeared in 1815 seems remarkable given the circumstances under which both brothers were working. While Jacob used every spare moment in Paris to copy manuscripts, Wilhelm in Cassel had to run a household, dealing with chimney fires and landlord conflicts. Wilhelm's letters reveal that his absent brothers were never far from his mind; he regularly checked the official lists of the dead and wounded, worried that he would spy a familiar name, and he was a faithful correspondent. To help meet household expenses, Wilhelm secured a position at court as secretary to the librarian, hoping over time to move into the second librarian's position. But even that didn't provide enough income to support the household, and after losing an appeal for lower rent, William moved everyone into a less expensive house. After a brief and joyous reunion in Cassel during late summer 1814, Jacob's government service took him to the Congress of Vienna for nearly a year and then to Paris to retrieve manuscripts and books from the Rhineland.

Jacob must have been effective in his official task in Paris, however, because the French said that they "could not endure that Monsieur Grimm, who comes and works here daily, and yet takes away our manuscripts.[15] The brothers' correspondence during these separations indicates that there may have been some warrant for rumors in the Hessian court that Jacob was spending more time on private research than on "living in society," as the *Landgraf* wanted him to do. The letters are filled with detailed exchanges about folk-tale motifs and manuscript variants, and Jacob had little time for Vienna's soirées, including literary parties such as Frau Schegel's salon. However, he met regularly with her husband, Friedrich von Schlegel, who had the means to help Jacob gain access to a rare codex of the *Nibelungenlied*.[16]

The titles of the Grimms' publications for 1815 and 1816 show the degree to which the brothers devoted time to their scholarship beyond the challenges of their official employment. In the Second Large Edition of the *Kinder-und Hausmärchen* volume 2 grew by seventy tales. Their edition of *Lieder der Alten Edda* (Songs of the Elder Edda, vol. 1, 1815) developed from their broader interest in Nordic literatures. Their *Deutsche Sagen* (German Legends, vol. 1, 1816) introduced a useful distinction between *Märchen* and legends; legends, they claimed, like the story of the Pied Piper of Hamelin or like many miracle tales and ghost stories, are tied to particular people, places, and times, whereas *Märchen* make no mention of historical particulars. In 1815 Jacob himself published a collection of old Spanish heroic poems, *Silva de Romances viejos* (Forest of Ancient Romances), which he did not translate because he believed that educated people ought to be able to read Spanish. *Irmenstrasse und Irmensäule* (Irmen Road and Irmen Pillar), a discussion of world-wide myth and folklore appeared in the same year.

After the turmoil of the Napoleonic wars, the brothers were happy to be able to spend several years living in peace in Cassel. Jacob regained his post as librarian to the court; Wilhelm, who otherwise would have been the likely candidate for the position, chose working with his brother over advancement.[17] Wilhelm also brought Jacob into Cassel's literary social life. In a reading group that included many who had contributed tales or legends to their collections they met weekly with devotees of folklore and literature. Jacob fit into this social world less well than Wilhelm; he preferred the stimulation provided by his own research. The project that he increasingly turned to over the next several years was his historical grammar of the German language. The first volume, dealing with inflection, appeared in 1819 and was remarkably well received, selling out its print run within a year. The work grew to four volumes over the next twenty years and made significant contributions to the study of linguistics.

While Jacob bent his primary scholarly energies toward grammar, Wilhelm gave his attention to a new edition of the *Kinder-und Hausmärchen*, beginning an editing process that he would continue until 1857. Excision (twenty-seven tales from the 1812 volume and seven from the 1815 volume), alteration (eighteen other tales combined old variants with newly collected ones), and addition (forty-five new tales) changed the collection, as did "genially help[ing]" the tales by altering elements within the tales.[18] Arnim and others had worried about the violence and sex in a number of the *Märchen*. Wilhelm said, "You can fool yourself into thinking that what can be removed from a book can also be removed from real life,"[19] but violence and sexual innuendo felt the cut of his editorial knife. Tales like "Children Who Played at Slaughtering," in which children butcher a playmate, were excised, and "Rapunzel," with its hints of premarital sex and pregnancy, was bowdlerized.[20]

With the brothers' increasing publications came academic recognition, membership in learned societies, and honorary degrees from the University of Marburg. The Grimms' connections broadened beyond their Cassel friends to include Sir Walter Scott, Wilhelm von Humboldt, Madame Schopenhauer, and August Wilhelm von Schlegel. Scholars visited from Sweden and Denmark, from France, England, and Eastern Europe. The brothers were offered professorships at Bonn University and elsewhere, but they turned them down because they wanted to continue their lives of quiet research. Recognition abroad was not matched by appreciation at home, however, where the Cassel court atmosphere became increasingly hostile.

Official hindrances did not slow down the Grimms' work. In 1822, Wilhelm put out a volume of notes to accompany the Second Large Edition of the *Kinder-und Hausmärchen,* and in 1825 he published an abridged version (Kleine Ausgabe) of fifty of the most popular tales with a handful of illustrations by his younger brother Ludwig Emil Grimm. Inspiration for this more marketable edition came in part from Edgar Taylor's English illustrated translation of the tales, *German Popular Stories* (1823), an edition that hugely outsold the Grimms' editions.[21]

In 1824 Jacob published a translation of the Serbian grammar that he had been working on since the Congress of Vienna, and in 1828 he published his important study of German law and custom, *Deutsche Rechtsalterthümer* (German Legal Antiquities), a work that inspired similar studies in France and the Netherlands. In 1826 Jacob and Wilhelm published *Irische Elfenmärchen,* a translation of Thomas Croker's *Fairy Legends and Traditions of the South of Ireland* and appended a substantial introduction on fairy tales that was later translated into English and added to the British edition. In 1829, Wilhelm completed what Jacob thought of as his brother's greatest achievement—*Die deutsche Heldensage* (German Heroic Tales)—acquainting readers with Germanic epics from the sixth through the sixteenth centuries.

The closeness of the brothers' relationship is perhaps never more striking to modern readers than in the years after Wilhelm's marriage to Dorothea Wild in 1825. Like Snow White in the household of the dwarfs, Dortchen, as Wilhelm affectionately called her, simply moved into the Grimms' bachelor household. As a neighbor and longtime friend whose family had supplied several tales to the *Kinder-und Hausmärchen*, she knew the Grimms well. A year later, Dortchen gave birth to a son, Jacob, but the child died before his first birthday. Their grief was tempered in 1828 by the birth of another son, Herman, who would grow up to be a literary historian. But Jacob, Wilhelm, and Dortchen's family life in Cassel was soon disrupted by court politics. Stung by being overlooked for promotion in the Cassel library, both brothers accepted positions at the University of Göttingen in the adjacent province of Hanover. The Landgraf's response revealed his ignorance of the brothers' reputation: "So the Grimms are leaving. What a loss! They have never done anything for me."[22]

The Göttingen years were turbulent for both brothers. On the one hand, their academic reputations grew stronger. Both were made corresponding members of the Academy of Sciences in Berlin, and in 1833 Jacob was appointed privy councillor to the king of Hanover. Wilhelm produced a Third Large Edition of the *Kinder-und Hausmärchen* (1837), as well as several critical editions of medieval works. Jacob put out a third volume of *Deutsche Grammatik* (1831); completed a project begun years before on his first trip to Paris, *Reinhart Fuchs* (Reynard the Fox, 1834), a long essay on tricksters and animal tales; and published his foundational study of myth and religion, *Deutsche Mythologie* (German Mythology, 1835). In addition, Wilhelm's family grew with the addition of a son, Rudolph, born in 1831, and a daughter, Auguste, born in 1832.

The Grimms' achievements came in the midst of significant challenges. Their sister, Lotte, died of complications from influenza, and Wilhelm's health was once again precarious: during much of 1834, he languished, the family feared, close to death. Similarly convinced of his imminent demise, the university awarded him a full professorship with a pension in 1835, in part, to provide for his wife and family in the event of his death. By 1836 Wilhelm began to recover, but both he and Jacob were troubled by the consequences of contemporary political events. Revolution again spread from France, and in Hanover, as throughout most of Germany's kingdoms, governments responded with repression. A spirit of censorship and suspicion entered the universities. On one research trip to Karlsruhe, Jacob's papers were seized and censored.

The brothers were thrust into the national limelight, when they and five other professors refused to sign allegiance to a new Hanoverian constitution that restricted the country's freedoms and that was instituted by the new king, Ernst August II. The king quickly fired all seven professors and, believing Jacob and two others to be the leaders of the group that came to be known as the Göttingen Seven, banished those three from the country. Students demonstrated, soldiers were sent to control the university, and three days later Jacob and the two other accused ringleaders were escorted to the Hanoverian-Hessian border by cavalry. The incident helped transform the Göttingen Seven into popular heroes, to whom groups of students and sometimes entire municipalities sent financial donations, while metal toys were manufactured to commemorate their border crossing.

Wilhelm and his family remained in Göttingen, while Jacob moved in with Ludwig Emil and his wife in Cassel. In 1838, Wilhelm's family joined Jacob and rented an apartment below their younger brother. For three years they remained unemployed, but upon the suggestion of a Leipzig publisher, they began work on what would become the *Deutsches Wörterbuch* (German Dictionary), inviting some fifty other scholars to join them in collecting examples of historical usage and etymology. For the rest of their lives they would work on this project, with the goal, as Wilhelm put it, to one day lay it "with pride and joy upon the altar of the fatherland" (Letter to Jacob Grimm, 6 April 1838 in Hennig, 238; trans. Hettinga). That was a joy that neither brother would experience, for the dictionary would not be completed until more than a century after their deaths, Wilhelm making it only through the letter *D* and Jacob extending their work just to the word *Frucht*.[23]

While they worked on the first five volumes of the dictionary in the final two decades of their lives, the brothers finally received both the recognition and the support that they deserved. In part through the intervention of their old friend Bettina von Arnim, the brothers became members of the Academy of Sciences in Berlin. No longer did they have to worry about income. The new king of Prussia, Friederich Wilhelm IV, promised them full support for their work on what his minister of education termed "the very great and difficult task which you have set yourselves in the completion of a complete critical dictionary of the German language."[24] The brothers gave occasional public lectures, a venue in which, as always, Wilhelm was the more comfortable. For his part, Jacob took on a public role in matters of German unity, presiding over the first two conferences of German philologists in 1846 and 1847. These meetings provided a forum for intellectuals interested in a unified Germany and thus were as significant politically as they were academically. He was elected to the 1848 Frankfurt Parliament, where he supported the movement toward constitutional government while sustaining amicable relations with the Prussian king, and hence exemplifying the paradoxical loyalties to individual freedom and aristocratic figures or institutions that characterized both brothers throughout their lives. Jacob's *Geschichte der deutschen Sprache* (History of the German Language), which appeared that year, is somewhat colored by contemporary nationalism.

Hans Christian Andersen visited the Grimms in 1844, but he was embarrassed to discover that Jacob had never heard of him. Wilhelm, who was out when Andersen called, *was* familiar with Andersen's tales, and the three had numerous contacts in subsequent years.[25]

The brothers' collaboration on the dictionary was in some ways less happy than that on other mutual projects. Wilhelm was frequently depressed, and Jacob, increasingly crotchety, was often irritated by Wilhelm's work habits and independence. Not only did Wilhelm not return books to their proper places on the shelves, complained Jacob, but he also made too much noise walking between their studies and was slow to agree with Jacob in instances where their opinions differed. On the whole, however, the brothers remained in an intimacy whose end brought Jacob a profound sense of loss. On 16 December 1859, two years after completing the last Large Edition of the *Kinder-und Hausmärchen*, Wilhelm died; and Jacob eulogized him in a lecture before the Berlin Academy in 1860.

Jacob continued to work on the dictionary and on the *Weisthümer* (Legal Precedents), a survey of German legal practices and common law, producing three additional volumes after Wilhelm's death. In the fall of 1863, after a brief holiday in the Harz mountains, Jacob grew ill, suffered a stroke, and died a few days later on 20 September 1863. According to Herman Grimm's account, one of Jacob's last actions was to gaze at a photograph of Wilhelm.[26]

Notes

1. Trans. Tatar, 253.
2. Briefwechsel, 80.
3. Jacob was born on 4 January 1785, and his brother was born almost exactly a year after on 24 February 1786.
4. Tatar, 260.
5. Ibid., 252–53.
6. Cf. Ward
7. Heinz Rölleke, "End of a Myth," 294.
8. Neumann, 31–32.

9. Tatar, 214.

10. Neumann, 33.

11. Rölleke, *KHM: 1856*, 3:563–65.

12. Bottigheimer, "Publishing History," 83.

13. Rölleke, *KHM: 1819*, 2:549–51.

14. *Briefwechsel*, 236.

15. Ibid., 450.

16. Ibid., 356–68.

17. Ibid., 472.

18. Rölleke 1982, 3:546–47; Steig, 319. See Bottigheimer, "Marienkind," for a case study of editorial change.

19. Tatar, 265.

20. Ibid., 18.

21. Bottigheimer, "Publishing History," 84.

22. Harder, 71.

23. Ibid., 114.

24. Hennig, 245.

25. Bredsdorff, 171.

26. Herman Grimm, 234.

Jacob and Wilhelm Grimm's Works

Books Published Jointly by the Brothers Grimm

Die beiden ältesten deutschen Gedichte aues dem achten Jahrhundert: Das Lied von Hildebrand und Hadubrand und das Weissenbrunner Gebet. Cassel: Thurneisen, 1812.

Kinder- und Hausmärchen. vol. 1, 1812; vol. 2, 1815. Second edition (2 vols.), 1819; vol. 3, 1822; *Kleine Ausgabe* (shorter edition) 1825; third edition (2 vols.), 1837; fourth edition (2 vols.), 1840; fifth edition (2 vols.), 1843; sixth edition (2 vols.), 1850; seventh edition (2 vols.), 1857.

Altdeutsche Wälder, vol. 1, 1813; vol. 22, 1815; vol. 3, 1816.

Der Arme Heinrich von Hartmann von der Aue, 1815.

*Lieder der Alten Edda,*vol. 1, 1815.

Deutsche Sagen, part 1, 1816; part 2, 1818.

Irischen Elfenmärchen, ed. Thomas Croften Croker, trans. from the English by the Brothers Grimm, 1826.

Books by Jacob Grimm

Über den altdeutschen Meistergesang, 1811.

Besinnungen aus meinem Leben, 1814.

Deutsches Worterbuch, von Jacob Grimm und Wilhelm Grimm. Leipzig: S. Hirzel, 1854–1971, 1 vol.

Irmenstrasse und Irmensäule. Eine mythologische Abhandlung von Jacob Grimm, 1815.

Silva de Romances viejos, 1815.

Deutsche Grammatik, vol. 1, 1819; vol. 2, 1826; vol. 3, 1831.

Wuk's Stephanowitsch kleine Serbische Grammatik verdeutsch und mit einer Vorrede von Jacob Grimm. Nebst Bermerkungen über die neuste Auffassung langer Heldenlieder aus dem Munde des Serbischen Volks, und der Übersicht des merkwürdigsten jener Lieder von Johann Severin Vater Vuk (Stefanovic Karadzic's Small Serbian Grammar Translated into German by and with a Forward by Jacob Grimm. Including remarks about the newest interpretation of Serbian oral epic heroic folk songs and the summary of the most remarkable features of each song by Johann Severin Vater), 1824.

Deutsche Rechtsaltertümer, 1828.

Reinhart Fuchs, 1834.

Deutsche Mythologie, 1835.

Über seine Entlassung, 1838.

Lateinische Gedichte des X. u. XI. Jahrhunderts, 1838.

Weistümer, vols. 1 and 2, 1840; vol. 3, 1842; vol. 4, 1863; vol. 5, 1866; vol. 6, 1869.

Geschichte der deutschen Sprache, 2 vols. 1848.

Books by Wilhelm Grimm

Altdänische Heldenlieder, Balladen und Märchen, trans. into German by Wilhelm Grimm, 1811.

Drei altschottische Lieder in Original und Übersetzung aus zwei neuen Sammlungen, 1813.

Über deutsche Runen, 1821.

Zur Literatur der Runen. Nebst Mittheilung runischer Alphabete und gothischer Fragmente aus Handschriften, 1828.

Grâve Rudolf, 1828.

Die deutsche Heldensage, 1829.

De Hildebrando antiquissimi carminis teutonici fragmentum edidit Guilelmus Grimm, 1830.

Vridankes Bescheidenheit, 1834.

Der Rosengarten, 1836.

Ruolandes liet, 1838.

Wernher von Niedderrhein, 1839.

Konrads von Würzburg Goldene Schmiede, 1840.

Konrads von Würzburg Silvester, 1841.

Über Freidank, 1855.

Secondary Literature

Bottigheimer, R. B. "'Marienkind' (KHM 3): A Computer-Based Study of Editorial Change and Stylistic Development within Grimms' Tales, 1808–1864." *ARV: Scandinavian Yearbook of Folklore* 46 (1990): 7–31.

Bottigheimer, Ruth B. *Grimms' Bad Girls and Bold Boys: The Moral and Social Vision of the Tales.* New Haven: Yale University Press, 1987.

——. "The Publishing History of the Grimms' Tales: Reception at the Cash Register." In *The Reception of Grimms' Fairy Tales: Responses, Reactions, Revisions,* ed. Donald Haase. Detroit: Wayne State University Press, 1993. 78–101.

Dundes, Alan. "Nationalistic Inferiority Complexes and the Fabrication of Fakelore: A Reconsideration of Ossian, the *Kinder-und Hausmärchen,* the *Kalevala,* and Paul Bunyan." *Journal of Folklore Research* 22 (1985): 5–18.

Ellis, John M. *One Fairy Story Too Many: The Brothers Grimm and Their Tales.* Chicago: University of Chicago Press, 1983.

Grimm, Herman. "The Brothers Grimm." *Essays on Literature.* Boston: Cupples and Hurd, 1888. 213–34.

Grimm, Jacob, and Wilhelm Grimm. *Briefwechsel zwischen Jacob und Wilhelm Grimm aus der Jugendzeit.* Ed. Wilhelm Schoof. Weimar: Hermann Böhlaus, 1963.

Harder, Hans-Bernd, and Ekkehard Kaufmann, eds. *Die Brüder Grimm in ihrer amtlichen und politischen Tätigkeit.* Kassel: Weber and Weidemeyer, 1985.

Hennig, Dieter, and Bernhard Lauer, eds. *Die Brüder Grimm: Dokumente ihres Lebens und Wirkens.* Kassel: Weber and Weidemeyer, 1985.

Hettinga, Donald R. *The Brothers Grimm: Two Lives, One Legacy.* New York: Clarion, 2001.

Michaelis-Jena, Ruth. *The Brothers Grimm.* New York: Praeger, 1970.

Neumann, Siegfried. "The Brothers Grimm as Collectors and Editors of German Folktales." In *The Reception of Grimms' Fairy Tales: Responses, Reactions, Revisions,* ed. Donald Haase. Detroit: Wayne State University Press, 1993. 24–40.

Reifferscheid, Alexander, ed. *Freundesbriefe von Wilhelm und Jacob Grimm.* Heilbronn: Gebr, Henniger, 1878.

Rölleke, Heinz, ed. *Kinder- und Hausmärchen: Nach der zweiten vermehrten und verbesserten Auflage von 1819.* 2 vols. Koln: Diederichs, 1982.

Rölleke, Heinz. "The 'Utterly Hessian' Fairy Tales by 'Old Marie': The End of a Myth." Trans. Ruth B. Bottigheimer. In *Fairy Tales and Society: Illusion, Allusion, and Paradigm,* ed. Ruth B. Bottigheimer. Philadelphia: University of Pennsylvania Press, 1986. 287–300.

Steig, Reinhold. *Achim von Arnim und Jacob und Wilhelm Grimm.* Stuttgart: Cotta, 1894.

Sutton, Martin. *The Sin-Complex: A Critical Study of English Versions of the Grimms' Kinder- und Hausmärchen in the Nineteenth Century.* Kassel: Brüder Grimm-Gesellschaft, 1996.

Tatar, Maria. *The Hard Facts of the Grimms' Fairy Tales.* 2nd ed. Princeton: Princeton University Press, 2003.

Ward Donald. "New Misconceptions about Old Folktales: The Brothers Grimm." In *The Brothers Grimm and Folktale,* ed. James M. McGlathery, et al. Urbana: University of Illinois Press, 1988. 91–99.

Ziolkowski, Jan M. *Fairy Tales from before Fairy Tales: The Medieval Latin Past of Wonderful Lies.* Ann Arbor: University of Michigan Press, 2007.

Zipes, Jack. "Once there were Two Brothers Named Grimm: A Reintroduction." In Jack Zipes, *The Brothers Grimm: From Enchanted Forests to the Modern World.* 2nd ed. New York: Palgrave Macmillan, 2002. 1–23.

———. *The Complete Fairy Tales of the Brothers Grimm.* 3rd ed. New York: Bantam, 2003.

Ludwig Bechstein

Ruth B. Bottigheimer

Ludwig Bechstein (1801–60), fathered by Louis Hubert Dupontreau, a French émigré from Fontenay-le-Comte in the French Vendée, was born on 24 November 1801 in Weimar to Johanna Karoline Dorothea Bechstein (1775–1847), the daughter of a minor official in Altenburg. Christened Louis Clairant Hubert Dupontreau, the baby was relinquished by his impoverished mother initially to a wigmaker's widow in Weimar, after whose death her unmarried daughter continued his care. His first eight years, Bechstein later remembered, were "a bad dream."[1]

Although young Louis's birth mother lived out her life in obscurity, her older, married brother Johann Matthäus Bechstein (1757–1822) was a well-known botanist, forester, and author of long-standard works on ornithology, entomology, and hunting, who also distinguished himself in education and local government. Devastated when his only son died at 18 in October 1810, Bechstein and his wife were advised to adopt a child to assuage their grief. Within weeks young Louis Dupontreau had been fetched to the small town of Dreissigacker, had been entered into the Dreissigacker Lyceum Illustre, and had changed his named to Ludwig Bechstein.

Bechstein's poor performance at the Meiningen lyceum occasionally resulted in the punishment of being forbidden to play outdoors. At those times he often listened to household servants tell local legends, in particular, he later remembered, ones about the nearby Hörsel Mountain. Neither talented for nor interested in academic study (whether of birds, animals, and trees, or of literature and history) young Bechstein instead ranged freely in the surrounding countryside by himself or with friends. When at home on his own, he devoured cheap adventure novels as well as serious works by now-classic authors such as E. T. A. Hoffmann, Friedrich Klopstock, and Friedrich Schiller. In the same period he also began composing verse.

Bechstein's formal schooling ended when he was apprenticed to a pharmacist in Arnstadt in the fall of 1818. Not yet seventeen, he found scrubbing floors, washing glassware, writing labels, and preparing and packaging apothecary products a disappointing employment. Nonetheless, Bechstein stayed the course, continued to write, and published verse when he was only eighteen.

When Bechstein completed his four-year apprenticeship in 1822, he remained in Arnstadt as a shop assistant two years longer. It was at this point that he developed a warm admiration for Johann Karl August Musäus (1735–1787), the late-eighteenth-century author who first portrayed literary fairy tales as a folk genre. (Herder had earlier written about *Volkspoesie* in discussing ballads.) Under the quasipseudonym C. Bechstein, he soon wrote and published a small volume of literary fairy tales that he, like Musäus, titled *Volksmährchen* (1823). In the following year Bechstein returned to Meiningen, worked in the court apothecary until 1826, and eventually rose to the position of apothecary dispenser in the employ of the Swan Apothecary in nearby Salzung.

From this point forward Bechstein devoted himself ever more single-mindedly to studying literature and writing poetry, the latter of which gained the attention of the Duke of Saxony-Meiningen, Bernhard II Ehrich Freund. After several personal encounters, Bechstein presented the Duke with a small volume of his verse, *Sonettenkränze* (1829), which led to his return to Meiningen and a lifelong association with the duke that was founded on shared interests.

At the age of twenty-eight, and with a ducal stipend, Bechstein began study at the University of Leipzig, attending lectures and seminars on philosophy, literature, and history. He gave early evidence for the breadth and depth of his interest in the German past (by joining the German Society for Researching the Language and Antiquities of the Fatherland) and of his own literary production (by composing an enormous number of novels, poems, novellas, legends, and imaginative works) in his student years. As a still young man, he summed up his approach to life as fulfilling one's duty and enjoying life to the fullest, "and if by God's grace he's a poet, he should take joy in his gift and use it."[2]

Bechstein remained in Leipzig through the 1830 summer semester and then moved to Munich, where he studied art and classical archaeology and made lifelong friends among the numerous artists, writers, and musicians whom he met there. Bechstein probably did not formally enroll at the university, for which—in any case—his social life and the fast pace of his writing would have left little time.

In the fall of 1831 Bechstein returned to Meiningen and entered ducal service as librarian and advisor, for which he was generously rewarded and variously employed. For instance, October 1831 found him reading his historical novel *Luther* aloud to the duke and his young son, and two months later Bechstein composed a theatrical prologue for the dedication of the newly constructed Meiningen theater that simultaneously celebrated the duke's birthday. He would subsequently write opera libretti for new productions there. Bechstein, a courtier as Basile and Perrault had been (although within a smaller court), routinely produced occasional verse for ducal birthdays, christenings, and special events. He also wrote plays and, from the mid-1830s onward, kept the duke apprised of the deliberations of the Meiningen Ducal Theater Commission, curated the ducal collections of paintings, coins, medals, and natural history, served as chief librarian of the ducal library, and undertook a systematic organization of the Meiningen archives. In his private life Bechstein founded the Meiningen-Henneberg Verein der Altertumsforschenden (Society for Researchers of Ancient History); remained its lifelong director; wrote numerous articles on historical subjects over the next thirty years; participated in local archaeology; and avidly collected German chapbooks, woodcuts (with a special interest in those depicting the Dance of Death), and local legends. Bechstein also traveled indefatigably in neighboring regions and gained an intimate knowledge of Thuringia, Bohemia, and Franconia.

As soon as Bechstein had a secure income, he married Caroline Wiskemann, whom he had come to know during his days as apothecary dispenser in Salzung. They had a son, Reinhold, before she died in 1834 at the age of twenty-six. About six months later Bechstein married Johanna Therese Schulz, with whom he ultimately had seven children.

Bechstein's literary output continued unabated, gaining the praise of one critic as a second Lord Byron![3] His diligence inevitably invites comparison with an equally productive contemporary, Jacob Grimm. In this connection his output must be accounted as a form of fluent and easily understood popular journalism, whereas Grimm's work tended towards the massively encyclopedic.

Bechstein's publicly expressed feelings about the Grimms underwent considerable change over the years. In 1838 (in a project he proposed to his Leipzig publisher Wigand) he viewed the Grimms' tales as a gold standard. Four years later, wishing to give concrete form to his admiration he proposed that the Meiningen-Henneberg Society for Researchers of Ancient History honor the Grimms as "absolutely the noblest caretakers of Old German and medieval German literature, verse, and knowledge";[4] and in 1844 he praised the Grimms' tales fulsomely, planning to produce an abridged version of their work. The Grimms, however, brusquely rebuffed Bechstein's editorial project, which impelled him to immediately set about assembling a collection of his own.

Completed within three short months,[5] Bechstein's *Deutsches Märchenbuch* (*German Folk and Fairy Tale Book*, 1845) was phenomenally successful, and with its title confidently changed to *Ludwig Bechsteins Märchenbuch* in 1853, it outsold the Grimms' collection until the 1890s.[6] Bechstein's collection of *Märchen*, like the Grimms', included numerous subgenres within the category of *Märchen*: parables, allegories, jests, animal tales, local legends, burlesques, wisdom tales, exemplary fables, and magic tales. Some he borrowed directly from the Grimm collection, others from tale collections published in the fifteenth through the nineteenth centuries. Bechstein's Enlightenment-influenced editing, however, diminished the proportion of wicked women, erased malevolent stepmothers as stock characters, and substituted community responsibility for individual guilt, alterations that changed the social implications of many tales. For his readership, he incorporated personal and social values that affirmed intact families, sibling loyalty, individual initiative, and—in the case of maternal death—positive portrayals of stepmothers. Bechstein also reformulated stories with Jewish protagonists so that violence against them was depicted both as a crime against an individual and as an infraction against the state. Even though Bechstein's tales aligned themselves with bourgeois society's reigning Enlightenment values, his comic criticisms of German schooling and his humorous portrayals of individuals such as a bearded and stertorous German parliamentarian or of values such as contemporary money grubbing allowed for and even encouraged ambivalence among adolescent readers toward standard social orthodoxies. It is worth mentioning that popular wall posters of the later nineteenth century overwhelmingly featured Bechstein's versions of standard tales rather than the Grimms'.[7]

Bechstein adopted a Herderian definition of fairy tales: a genre that had evolved from the childhood of humanity and was therefore

proper for the childhood of individuals. With formulaic language, prov-
erbs, and Bible citations, his tales paralleled contemporary usage, while
his frequent notation "*mündlich*" (oral) referred to public knowledge of
the tales in question, rather than to oral sources.

For the newly titled 1853 edition, Bechstein engaged a popular
illustrator, Ludwig Richter (1803–84), who produced scores of charming
woodcuts. In his 1853 foreword Bechstein expressed the desire that his
collection be a *Volksbuch* (book for the people), and at half the price of
the Grimms' two-volume edition of *Kinder-und Hausmärchen*,[8] Bechstein's
tales were eminently affordable.

Like the Grimms, Bechstein understood Germany's folk and fairy
tales to have emerged from a broadly sweeping national epic, his views
of which were strongly colored by his and his bourgeois contemporaries'
Enlightenment values. Thus for Bechstein, Germany's "folk" meant not
a minimally literate and undereducated class of manual workers, but the
entire population of every social class. It was for this inclusive population
that he wrote *Germania: Die Vergangenheit, Gegenwart und Zukunft der
deutschen Nation* (*Germania: The Past, Present, and Future of the German
Nation*, 1851), in which he took a broad social view of national history.
In 1854 he published two books. One—*Das deutsche Volk dargestellt in
Vergangenheit und Gegenwart zur Begründung der Zukunft* (*The German
People Portrayed in the Past and the Present for the Purpose of a Foundation for the Future*)—similarly considered the German population as a
whole, while the other—*Zweihundert deutsche Männer in Bildnissen und
Lebensbeschreibungen* (*Two Hundred German Men in Portraits and Biogra-
phies*)—provided thumbnail sketches of national cultural heroes.

In the mid-1840s Bechstein had reorganized the archives of Hen-
neberg, a county whose ancient Thuringian roots were related to the
powerful medieval Babenbergs. This work led to his 1848 appointment
as *Hofarchivist* (court archivist) and deepened his historical sensibilities.
When revolution swept Europe in 1848, he initially ranged himself with
reformers, but soon stepped back from political controversy because of
what he perceived as an offensively unbalanced radicalism.

Throughout the 1840s and 1850s Bechstein continued to write
on a broad range of subjects: the natural history of caged birds, travel,
literature, folk belief, and history, as well as a lengthy appreciation of
his stepfather's life and career. His birth mother lived until 1847 and
saw the son she had had to give up become a nationally known figure.

In 1855 Bechstein was entrusted with the responsibility of accompanying Meiningen's Crown Prince Georg on a tour of northern Italy.

Fifty-four years old, he was at the height of his professional and personal career, a happily married father of a large family, a passionate collector, and a prosperous Meiningen householder whose home drew visitors from near and far who came to meet and pay homage to this well-known man.

Bechstein's second popular tale collection, *Das neue deutsche Märchenbuch* (*The New German Folk and Fairy Tale Book*), was published in Pest, Vienna, and Leipzig in 1856. In its preface he openly denominated the changes he made to various fairy tales in the collection as well as giving his reasons for doing so.[9] This volume also met popular acceptance, reaching its 105th printing in 1922. Despite the fact that Bechstein's versions of tales that appeared in both Bechstein's and the Grimms' collections were the better known, and despite the fact that Bechstein's collections outsold the Grimms' collection for the first fifty years of their existence, that situation changed abruptly when the respective copyrights lapsed in the 1890s. At that point, commercial competition and social change together moved the popularity of the Grimm collection ahead of those of Bechstein. Numerous publishers leapt into the market, issuing cheaply priced Grimm editions, while an influential early-twentieth-century teachers' journal, *Jugendschriften-Warte*, denounced Bechstein as bourgeois and alien, while praising the Grimms as providers of true "folk" readings. A nationalist educational polemicist, Franz Heyden bitterly opposed Bechstein's underlying Enlightenment ethic and attacked his tales as un-German with "no right to exist," sentiments that undermined sales. When post–World War I educationists and politicians publicly and loudly redefined German identity as folk-based, Bechstein's tales took a distant second place to the now dominant Grimm collection.

Bechstein became ill in November 1859, declined new responsibilities, but continued writing through the late winter and spring of 1860: a history of astrology; a treatise on the phantasmagorical arts; a folktale; and his last work, a description and analysis of German folk humor as it emerges in images of death and the iconic dance of death. Bechstein died on 14 May 1860, not yet fifty-nine years old, and was buried in the Park Cemetery in Meiningen, having enjoyed public acclaim to the end of his life.

For many decades public and scholarly interest in Bechstein was limited to a few dissertations and articles, but the bicentenary of his birth produced renewed interest in the kaleidoscopic interests of his universal enthusiasms and achievements.[10]

Notes

1. Mederer, *Stoffe*, 1.
2. Letter to Ludwig Storch, 9 April 1830, cited in Mederer, *Stoffe*, 4.
3. Mederer, *Stoffe*, 7.
4. Bechstein, *Mythe, Sage, Märe und Fabel im Leben und Bewusstsein des deutschen Volkes* (226–27), claiming their work as "a worthy pattern" (228).
5. Uther, "Ludwig Bechstein und seine Märchen," 32.
6. Bottigheimer, "The Publishing History of Grimms' Tales," 85–87.
7. Uther, "Ludwig Bechstein und seine Märchen," 46–47; Bottigheimer, "Ludwig Bechstein's Fairy Tales."
8. Uther, "Ludwig Bechstein und seine Märchen," 35.
9. Ibid., 40.
10. See, above all, the essays by more than twenty scholars in the two-volume *Ludwig Bechstein: Dichter, Sammler, Forscher: Festschrift zum 200*, ed. Jakob and Seifert (2001).

Ludwig Bechstein's Works*

Tales

Thüringische Volksmärchen (Thuringian Folk Tales). Sondershausen: C. Fleck, 1823.

Mährchenbilder und Erzählungen. Leipzig: Magazin für Industrie und Literatur, [1829].

Nala und Damajanti: Indische Mährchen für die Jugend (Nala and Damajanti: Indian Fairy Tales for the Young). Stuttgart: Eduard Hallberger, 1831.

Die Volkssagen und Legenden des Kaiserstaates Oesterreich (The Folk Legends and Myths of Imperial Austria). Leipzig: C. B. Polet, 1840.

Deutsches Märchenbuch (German Folk and Fairy Tale Book). Leipzig: G. Wigand, 1845.

Hexengeschichten (Witch Stories). Halle: C. C. M. Pfeffer, 1854.

Romantische Märchen (Romantic Fairy Tales). Altenburg: H. A. Pierer, 1855.

Märchen und Sagen für Jung und Alt (Fairy Tales and Legends for Young and Old). Düsseldorf: n.p., 1856.

Neues Deutsches Märchenbuch (New German Folk and Fairy Tale Book). Vienna / Pest / Leipzig: Hartleben, 1856.

---

*Bechstein wrote so prolifically that it is neither possible nor desirable to list his entire oeuvre. Listed by genre, his most important works follow.

Recent Editions

Ludwig Bechstein. Deutsches Märchenbuch. Frankfurt am Main / Leipzig: Insel, 1993.

Deutsches Märchenbuch. Stuttgart: P. Reclam, 1996.

Ludwig Bechstein. Deutsches Märchenbuch. Nach der Ausgabe von 1857, textkritisch revidiert und durch Register erschlossen. Ed. Hans-Jörg Uther. Munich: Eugen Diederichs, 1997.

Tales Translated into English

The Old Story-Teller: Popular German Tales Collected by Ludwig Bechstein. London: Addey, 1854.

As Pretty as Seven and Other Popular German Tales: A Companion to Grimm's Popular Stories. London: J. C. Hotten, 1872, 1884, 1986.

An Easy German Reader, With Full Vocabulary. Ed. S. Tindall and J. D.E.Williams. London: Bell, 1928.

The Rabbit Catcher and Other Fairy Tales. Trans. Randall Jarrell. New York: Macmillan, 1961, 1962.

Fairy Tales. Trans. A. Bell. London: Abelard-Schuman, 1967.

Popular Studies

"Das Märchen und seine Behandlung in Deutschland." *Germania* 2 (1852): 316–28.

Mythe, Sage, Märe und Fabel im Leben und Bewusstsein des deutschen Volkes (Myth, Legend, Tale, and Story in the Life and Awareness of the German People). Leipzig: T. D. Weigel, 1854.

Correspondence

Schmidt-Knaebel, Susanne. "Man muss doch jemand haben, gegen den man sich ausspricht"—Ludwig Bechsteins Briefe an Dr. Ludwig Storch. Aachen: Shaker Verlag, 2000 (=Berichte aus der Literaturwissenschaft).

Weigel, Heinrich. *Ludwig Bechstein in Briefen an Zeitgenossen.* Frankfurt am Main / New York: Lang, 2007.

Archives

Nachlass Alexander Kaufmann: Fürstliches Löwenstein'sche Archiv (Wertheim am Main).

Nachlass Bechstein: Goethe-Schiller Archiv (Weimar) has the manuscript of Bechstein's "Summa summarum" (published in *Ludwig Bechsteins Märchenbuch.* Leipzig / Weimar: G. Kiepenheuer, 1984.

Nachlass Friedrich Hoffmann: Landesbibliothek (Coburg).
Staatsbibliothek (Berlin).
Nachlass Fromann: Germanisches Nationalmuseum (Nürnberg).

Secondary Literature

Boost, K. "Ludwig Bechstein." Diss. Würzburg 1926.

Bottigheimer, Ruth B. "Ludwig Bechstein's Fairy Tales: Nineteenth-Century Bestsellers and Bürgerlichkeit." *Internationales Archiv für Sozialgeschichte der deutschen Literatur* 15.2 (1990): 55–88.

———. "The Publishing History of Grimms' Tales: Reception at the Cash Register." 78–101 in *The Reception of Grimms' Fairy Tales: Responses, Reactions, Revisions,* ed. Donald Haase. Detroit: Wayne State University Press, 1993.

———. "Ludwig Bechstein (1801–1860): Deutsches Märchenbuch. Leipzig 1845." Otto Brunken / Bettina Hurrelmann / Klaus-Ulrich Pech, eds. *Handbuch zur Kinder- und Jugendliteratur. Von 1800 bis 1850.* Stuttgart: Metzler, 1998: 977–993.

———. "Bechstein, Ludwig." *Oxford Companion to Fairy Tales,* ed. Jack Zipes. New York: Oxford University Press, 2000. 49–50.

Fiedler, Alfred. "Ludwig Bechstein als Sagensammler und Saganpublizist." *Deutsches Jahrbuch für Volkskunde* 12 (1966):243–266.

Heyden, Franz. "Grimm oder Bechstein? Zur Kritik der Bechsteinschen Märchen." Jugendschriften-Warte 6 (1908):13–15; 8(1908): 22–24.

Jakob, A., Andreas Seifert, and Ludwig Bechstein. *Ludwig Bechstein: Dichter, Sammler, Forscher: Festschrift zum 200. Geburtstag.* Meiningen: Kloster Vessra: Meininger Museen in der Kulturstiftung Meiningen, 2001. 2 vols. (= *Jahrbuch des Hennebergisch-Fränkischer Geschichtsverein* 16.1–2.

Linschmann, T. *Ludwig Bechsteins Schriften.* Meiningen: Brückner & Renner, 1907.

Mederer, Hanns-Peter. *Stoffe aus Mythen: Ludwig Bechstein als Kulturhistoriker, Novellist und Romantiker.* Wiesbaden: Deutscher Universitäts-Verlag, 2002.

———, ed. *Ludwig Bechstein's Briefe an Friedrich Wilhelm von Kawaczinski. Die Hoftheater Meiningen und Coburg-Gotha, 1831–1848.* Bad Langensalza: Verlag Rockstuhl, 2007.

Richter, Karin and Rainer Schlundt, eds. *Lebendige Märchen- und Sagenwelt. Ludwig Bechsteins Werk im Wandel der Zeiten.* Baltmannsweiler: Schneider Verlag Hohengehren GmbH, 2003.

Uther, Hans-Jörg. "Ludwig Bechstein und seine Märchen. Zur Bedeutung des Märchens um die Mitte des 19. Jahrhunderts." *Palmbaum: Literarisches Journal aus Thüringen* 9.1–2 (2001): 29–53.

———. "Bechstein, Ludwig." *Greenwood Encyclopedia of Folktales & Fairy Tales,* ed. Donald Haase. Westport CT: Greenwood Press, 2008. 109–111.

VI

Sentimentalization

Andersen
Nineteenth-Century Denmark

Hans Christian Andersen

Peer E. Soerenscn

Born in poverty in 1805, Hans Christian Andersen became world famous in his lifetime, with his works, especially the fairy tales, translated into 125 languages. He realized the modern myth of upward mobility and paraded it far and wide. He received numerous medals and honors and left behind a major literary oeuvre and a fortune when he died in 1875. Hans Christian Andersen was more than a fairy-tale writer: he also composed dramas and comedies, novels, travel books, poems, stories, letters, and diaries and produced drawings and paper collages.

Even though Andersen wrote from the beginning of his life to the very end, his writings do not illuminate his life. Hans Christian Andersen did not develop into an enlightened and mature author like Wolfgang von Goethe, who served as an example for Danish authors of the time. In the fairy tales, the reader finds neither a leitmotiv nor a solid and consistent sense of self. On the contrary, his fairy-tale collections are highly complex and contain a mixture of many narrative forms. Even though he repeatedly uses the same themes, the results vary aesthetically and existentially. In collection after collection his fairy tales are discontinuous and inconsistent with one another; as optimistic and harmonious fairy tales are placed alongside others in which harmony is distorted or subverted. The tales' childlike tone cannot obscure a world of adult contradictions that govern his production of fairy tales.

Andersen's work, a sustained self-representation, is set somewhere between his impoverished childhood in a provincial town and his adult life among the aristocratic bourgeoisie in the capital of Denmark, two extremes about which he always felt personal reservations. Ambivalence is a hallmark of his writing: he praises the noble world of which he wanted to be a part and valorizes the poverty into which he was born. These irresolvable contradictions make Hans Christian Andersen an ironic narrator in the manner of the German romanticists E. T. A Hoffmann, Adalbert von Chamisso, and Ludwig Tieck. At the same time he is also a homiletic defender of the aristocratic culture of cultivated education as exemplified by Goethe and a dreamer who, like Jean-Jacques Rousseau, wanted to escape to a fictitious childhood. It is a paradox in Andersen's work that, despite its autobiographic content, he always concealed himself, his writing a permanent mask.

Andersen was born in Odense, then a small town of six thousand inhabitants, in April 1805. He died in Copenhagen in August 1875 and was buried in Assistens Cemetery. The son of Hans Andersen, a poor shoemaker, and Anne Marie Andersdatter, who earned her living as a washerwoman, Andersen's childhood was marked by deep poverty and social marginality. His grandfather, Anders Hansen Traes, ended his life as an insane eccentric on the streets of Odense. His grandmother, in trying to convince him that he was of noble descent, contributed to creating the myth that he—a great genius—was a prince or nobleman. Scholars today have dismissed this possibility, but Andersen himself might have believed it.

Andersen's father's uncommon interests included reading Shakespeare, the Danish Enlightenment author Ludvig Holberg, and *Thousand and One Nights*. In his memoirs, Andersen asserts that his father read to him and told him stories and in this way instilled a love of fiction in the little boy's imagination. Andersen depicts his father, who tried to escape from poverty as a soldier, but died in 1816 without doing so, in his 1837 novel *Kun en Spillemand* (Only a Fiddler).

Andersen was attached to his mother. In spite of her increasing alcoholism, she took care of her son, who for his part never forgot her. In the fairy tale "Hun duede ikke" ("She Was Good for Nothing"), he staunchly defends a washerwomen who resembles his mother against the contemptuous and disdainful glances of the upper class. Before marrying his father she had borne a daughter, his half-sister, Karen Marie, whom Andersen mentioned only in the novel *OT* (short for *Odense Tugthus*, meaning the Prison of Odense, 1836). She apparently represented a traumatized and suppressed domain of his consciousness. In his imagination she was a demonic figure beyond his control, and he always feared meeting her on the streets of Copenhagen, where she earned a living. Andersen certainly did not love scandals, and he disliked being reminded of his origins—unless he did so himself.

As a child, Andersen attended the charity school in Odense. Not a hard-working pupil, he preferred doing puppet theater and sewing puppet clothing. At least, that is what he asserts in his memoirs, and that assertion shows one way in which he promoted himself and used his childhood as a major source for his work. A fairy-tale-like "Stormen flytter Skilt" ("The Storm Shifts the Signboards") demonstrates a subtle sensitivity and suggests a host of childhood experiences in Odense. He heard many fairy tales in the town poorhouse, but it was not the only source for his rich store of memories.

In 1819, after his religious confirmation, he decided to go to Copenhagen to become an actor. It seems an ill-conceived project, for he had very little money. At the outset he encountered one setback after another. He tried acting, singing, and dancing, but his awkward body and poor coordination suited him poorly for these activities. In addition, his singing voice disappeared rapidly with the onset of puberty. He also tried his hand at writing comedies, which revealed few flashes of talent, but which helped him gain patronage. Hans Christian OErsted; a physician, philosopher, and professor; Admiral Wulff, the translator of Shakespeare; and Jonas Collin, the president of the Royal Theatre and one of the most prominent public servants in Copenhagen at the time, became his protectors, the Collin family remaining so until the end of Andersen's life. To remedy Andersen's deficient education, Jonas Collin placed him in a Latin school in a small town and obtained royal support for his studies. Unfortunately, the school, where the pedantic and sadistic headmaster persecuted him, was a hellish experience. The letters he sent from there reveal a dismayed defeatism and a severe lack of self-confidence. In 1827, Jonas Collin moved him to Copenhagen, where with the help of private tutoring he matriculated in 1828. Andersen described his school years with clear-eyed realism in his first memoir, Levnedsbogen (Autobiography), and the sadistic headmaster lived on in many self-satisfied and narrow-minded pedants in his fairy tales.

In 1827 he published a collection of poems, which pointed the way toward his future life but as an author. His first book, Fodreise fra Holmens Kanal til OEstpynten af Amager (Journey on Foot from Holmens Kanal to the Eastern Point of Amager, 1829), was a satirical, ironic, and successful travel book in the manner of the German romanticists Jean Paul and E. T. A. Hoffmann. The same year he published minor dramatic works and several collections of poems that demonstrate a multitude of inspirations, but no dedicated commitment. A journey to Germany in 1831 resulted in *Skyggebilleder af en Rejse til Hartzen og det sachsiske Schweitz* (Rambles in the Romantic Regions of the Hartz Mountains and Saxon Switzerland).

In April 1833 Andersen received a travel grant and immediately left Copenhagen for Italy. He arrived in Rome in October 1833, where he was aided by Bertel Thorvaldsen, a prominent Danish sculptor, who appears in the dignified and benign count in "Portnerens Soen" "(The Porter's Son"), as well as in several other fairy tales. Like most artists and authors of his day, Andersen visited Naples, Vesuvius, Capri, and Venice before returning to Copenhagen in 1834.

The trip to Italy released the young Andersen from the pressure of Copenhagen's social establishment and at the same time provided him with new and exotic themes. In the novel *Improvisatoren* (The Improvisator, 1835) the protagonist is an only slightly altered representation of Andersen. His descriptions of Italian people and landscapes radiate the author's curiosity and keen powers of observation. A stylistic liberation from the academic tradition in Danish prose, it also anticipated the free style of his later fairy tales. The novel, an immediate international success, grounded his literary reputation.

Later in the 1830s he wrote several novels, all of which were translated into many languages. *OT* (1836) and *Kun en Spillemand* (1837) are both autobiographical. Andersen's sentimental description of the protagonist in *Kun en Spillemand* irritated the philosopher Soeren Kierkegaard, who insulted and disdained the novelist in his pamphlet *Af en endnu Levendes Papirer* (From the Papers of Someone Still Living, 1838). Although these two geniuses never came to understand each other, Andersen's works were nevertheless disseminated and read by others all over Europe. In 1839 the collection *Billedbog uden Billeder* (A Picture Book without Pictures) consolidated his literary reputation throughout Europe. He had earned respect in Denmark too, receiving a lifetime pension from the state. Although his dramas experienced success in his own day, they are seldom read today. Later he published the novels *De to Baronesser* (The Two Baronesses, 1848), *At være eller ikke være* (To Be or Not to Be, 1857), and *Lykke-Peer* (Happy Peer, 1870).

From 1840 to 1873 Andersen, one of the first great travelers in European literature, traveled abroad thirty times, establishing acquaintances in countless circles. Restless and with a sense of being more or less in exile most of his life, he felt at home everywhere and nowhere. "To travel is to live," he wrote, and thereby created a formula for modern, rootless lives. His travels inspired a series of brilliant travel books, such as *I Sverige* (Pictures of Sweden, 1851), and *En Digters Bazar* (A Poet's Bazaar, 1842), which describes his journey to the orient in 1840 and 1841.

Eventually, Andersen's fame made his travels into spectacular triumphal processions. Poets, noblemen, and princes vied with each other in praising him. He knew Victor Hugo, Alphonse de Lamartine, Alfred de Vigny, Honoré de Balzac, Alexandre Dumas, Heinrich Heine, Ludwig Tieck, and Charles Dickens. He frequented the houses of princes, became an intimate friend of Archduke Carl Alexander of Sachsen-Weimar, accepted the Danish King Christian VIII's invitation to court, and toured Danish manor houses. However great his public success, he still suffered from personal uncertainty and growing hypochondria. He straightened out his financial circumstances, but not the turbulence in his soul. One might say, "To write is to live." Hans Christian Andersen lived more confidently in his writing than in his life.

Andersen began writing fairy tales in 1835, eventually composing 156 of them. The first collection (1835) contains four of the best-known: "Fyrtoeiet" ("The Tinder Box"), "Lille Claus og Store Claus" ("Little Claus and Big Claus"), "Prindsessen paa Ærten" ("The Princess on the Pea"), and "Den lille Idas Blomster" ("Little Ida's Flowers"). "Fyrtoeiet" and "Lille Claus og Store Claus" are based on folktales, while the others were invented by Andersen himself. In an age that perceived fairy tales as magical and otherworldly, Andersen maintained a mixture of folktales and literary fairy tales, as the Grimms had done.

From the very beginning Andersen had a conscious strategy for his narratives, which he elaborated in a letter to a colleague: "I have written these fairy tales in the same manner that I would tell them to children." Andersen knew well the difference between the oral genres that had inspired him and the written narrative that he created. He broke with the traditional academic style by creating a hybrid between the oral and written forms. By simultaneously narrating for children and maintaining an adult consciousness, he found a writing strategy that freed both his stylistic skills and his imagination from traditional literary styles. Like the Grimms, Andersen imitated childlike expressions and everyday usage and idioms, but his style is marked by a complex tone. Critics were, in part rightly, skeptical and had moral scruples about the tales' multivalence. Told to children, Andersen's stories are certainly not only for children, often balancing on the edge of decorum. Two pamphlets in a series entitled *Eventyr, fortalte for Boern* (Fairy Tales Told for Children) appeared in 1835 and 1837 and closed the first period of Andersen's writing of fairy tales.

From 1838 to 1842 Andersen composed a new collection in which one finds many of his most renowned fairy tales: "Den lille Havfrue" ("The Little Mermaid"), "Reisekammeraten" ("The Traveling Companion"), "Keiserens nye Klæder" ("The Emperor's New Clothes"), "Den standhaftige Tinsoldat" ("The Steadfast Tin Soldier"), "Ole Lukoeie" ("Ole Lukoie"), and "Svinedrengen" ("The Swineherd"). Subsequently, he published *Nye Eventyr* (*New Fairy Tales*) between 1845 and 1848 and *Historier* (*Stories*) 1–2 between 1852 and 1853.

Andersen's collections differ from those of Peter Asbjoernson and Jorgen Moe in Norway, of Svend Grundtvig in Denmark, and of Jacob and Wilhelm Grimm in Germany, because he invented all the fairy tales in these books except "Klods Hans" ("Clumsy Hans") and created his own personal narrative forms by simulating an oral narrative tone that differs from both the folktale and the German romantic literary fairy tale. Andersen used the subtitle "Told for Children" only in the early collections. Andersen's fairy tales comprise traditional narrative forms and include trolls and supernatural events as well as realistic everyday stories that anticipate later realistic literary trends in Denmark. "De rode Sko" ("The Red Shoes") is a harsh story about guilt, sexuality, and punishment; "Hjertesorg" ("Heartache") is an ironic text about the relativity of feelings and contains subtle metapoetic reflections, as does "Tante Tandpine" ("Aunty Toothache"). Side by side with these modern texts are pious religious stories like "Verdens deiligste Rose" ("The Worlds Fairest Rose") and "Hoerren" ("The Flax"). In "Sneedronningen" ("The Snow Queen"), he tries to eliminate the reign of the devil through a child's naiveté. Tragic and comic love stories like "Hyrdinden og Skorstensfeieren" ("The Shepherdess and the Chimneysweep") stand alongside a homage to the world exhibition in Paris in 1867 in "Dryaden" ("The Dryad"). "Nattergalen" ("The Nightingale"), a brilliant story about art as a liberating, divine force originating in childlike poverty, allegorizes his own life. Like the poor girl in the fairy tale, he, a well-known author, offers the life-giving fairy tale to his artificial and superficial contemporaries. "Grantræet" ("The Fir Tree") and "Den grimme Ælling" ("The Ugly Duckling") also illustrate how he viewed himself as well as how he incorporated biographical elements into his tales, themes that recur in his 1847 autobiography, *Das Märchen meines Lebens ohne Dichtung* (The True Story of my Life). *Mit Livs Eventyr* (The Fairy Tale of my Life, 1855; United States 1869) also outlines divine guidance from poverty and darkness to richness and light.

Besides memoirs, Andersen also regularly kept a diary and corresponded with scores of people. In the Danish version of the German autobiography, *Mit Livs Eventyr uden Digtning* (The Fairy Tale of my Life without Fiction), he describes himself with the following pathetic words: my life "is a beautiful fairy tale. It is so rich and happy! Had I met a mighty fairy when I went poor and lonely out in the world as a little boy, and if the fairy had said to me: Do what you want to do. Follow your spirit, and I will protect and guide you, nothing could have been more happy, more clever and better, than it is. The story of my life will tell the world what it tells me: there is a mighty God who leads everything to the best." This divine hope is manifested in several fairy-tales such as "Skrubtudsen" ("The Toad") and "Klokken" ("The Bell"), but this is something in which he did not always trust.

In the last years of Andersen's long and productive life he devoted himself principally to the fairy-tale genre. Between 1858 and 1872, he published the three-volume *Nye Eventyr og Historier* (New Fairy Tales and Stories), whose title suggests the book's narrative diversity. "Story" implies narratives without fairy-tale elements but with an oral tone. The collections contain thematically heterogeneous texts, such as the lyric "Vinden fortæller om Valdemar Daa og hans Doetre" ("The Wind Tells about Valdemar Daae and His Daughters"), the ironic and playful "Hvad Fatter gioer er altid det rigtige" ("What the Old Man Does Is Always Right"), "Laserne" ("The Rags") and "Nissen og Madammen" ("The Goblin and the Woman"), metapoetic fairy tales like "Tante Tandpine," and the carnivalesque "Elverhoei" ("The Elf Mound"). "Kroeblingen" ("The Cripple"), his last fairy tale, pathetically recapitulates his fragile belief in harmony and reconciliation, as poverty disappears and God's guidance is fully evident and as nature, poverty, and religion comprise a cosmic harmony for the last time in Danish literature. The story dreams of happiness but contains a huge portion of sorrow and despair. It was a dream of happiness that Andersen never realized in his own life except when he wrote about it. His authorship was his true home, his castle.

Hans Christian Andersen's Works

Novels

Fodreise fra Holmens Kanal til OEstpynten af Amager. N.p.: N.p., 1829 (not translated).

Improvisatoren. Copenhagen: C. A. Reitzel, 1835 (*The Improvisatore; or, Life in Italy.* London: R. Bentley, 1845).

OT. 1836 (*OT, or Life in Denmark.* London and New York, 1845).

Kun en Spillemand. Copenhagen: C. A. Reitzel, 1837 (*Only a Fiddler.* London: R. Bentley/New York: Harper, 1845).

De to Baronesser. Copenhagen: n.p., 1848 (*The Two Baronesses.* London: R. Bentley, 1848).

At være eller ikke være. Copenhagen: C. A. Reitzel, 1857 (*To Be or Not to Be.* London: R. Bentley, 1857).

Lykke-Peer. Copenhagen: C. A. Reitzel, 1870 (translated as *Lykke-Per,* 1871).

Memoirs

Das Märchen meines Lebens ohne Dichtung, 1847 (*The True Story of my Life.* London: Longman, Brown, Green, and Longmans/Boston: J. Munroe and Co, 1847).

Mit Livs Eventyr. Copenhagen: C. A. Reitzel, 1855 (American edition 1869, *The True Story of My Life*).

Levnedsbogen. Copenhagen: N.p., 1926 (not translated).

Travel Books

Skyggebilleder af en Reise til Hertzen og det sachsiske Schweitz. Copenhagen: C. A. Reitzel, 1831 (English translation: *Rambles in the Romantic Regions of the Hartz Mountains, Saxon Switzerland.* London: R. Bentley, 1848).

En Digters Bazar. Copenhagen: N.p., 1842 (*A Poet's Bazaar.* London: R. Bentley, 1846).

I Sverige. Copenhagen: C. A. Reitzel, 1851 (*Pictures of Sweden.* London: R. Bentley, 1851).

I Spanien. Copenhagen: C. A. Reitzel, 1863 (*In Spain.* London: N.p., 1864/New York: Hurd, 1870).

Et Besoeg I Portugal, 1868 (*A Visit to Portugal 1866.* London 1972).

Fairy Tales and Stories

Eventyr, fortalte for Boern (*Fairy Tales Told for Children*). Copenhagen: C. A.Reitzel, 1835–42.

Billedbog uden Billeder. Copenhagen: C. A. Reitzel, 1839 (*A Picture Book without Pictures.* London: David Bogue, 1847).
Nye Eventyr. Copenhagen: C. A. Reitzel, 1845–48.
Historier I–II. Copenhagen: C. A. Reitzel, 1852–53.
Nye Eventyr og Historier, 1–3. Copenhagen: C. A. Reitzel, 1858–72.
H. C. Andersens Eventyr. Kritisk udgivet efter de originale Eventyrhæfter, 7 vols. Copenhagen: C. A. Reitzel, 1963–67.
Hans Christian Andersen: The Complete Stories. Trans. Jean Hersholt. Preface Brian Alderson. London: The British Library, 2005.

Plays and Operas

Maurerpigen. N.p.: N.p., 1840 (not translated).
Mulatten. Copenhagen: C. A. Reitzel, 1840 (not translated).
Liden Kirsten. Copenhagen: C. C. Lose and Delbanco, 1846 (not translated).

Poetry

Phantasier og Skizzer. Copenhagen: C. A. Reitzel, 1831 (not translated).
Samlede Digte. Copenhagen: C. A. Reitzel, 1833 (not translated); *Samlede Digte.* Copenhagen: Aschehoug, 2000.
Digte, gamle og nye. Copenhagen: C. A. Reitzel, 1847 (not translated).
Fædrelandske Vers og Sange under Krigen. Copenhagen: C. A. Reitzel, 1851 (not translated).

Collected Works

Samlede Skrifter, 33 vols. Copenhagen: C. A. Reitzel, 1853ff. (incomplete).
Digte: der ikke kom med I eventyrdigterens "Samlede Skrifter." Copenhagen: Joergen Skjerk, 2003. (new and complete edition).

Correspondence

Breve til Hans Christian Andersen. Udgivne af C.St.A. Bille og Nikolaj Boegh. Copenhagen: C. A. Reitzel, 1877.
Breve fra Hans Christian Andersen. Udgivne af C. St.A. Bille og Nikolaj Boegh. 2 vols. Copenhagen: C. A. Reitzel, 1878.
Breve til og fra H. C. Andersen. Copenhagen: C. A. Reitzel, 1877–78 (incomplete).
H. C. Andersens Brevveksling med Edvard og Henriette Collin. Udgivet af C. Behrend og H. Topsoe-Jensen. 6 vols. Copenhagen: Levin and Munksgaard, 1933–37.
Nielsen, Birger Frank: *H. C. Andersen Bibliografi. Digterens danske Værker 1822–1875,* Copenhagen: H. Agerup, 1942 (online at: http://www.andersen.sdu.dk).

H. C. Andersens Brevveksling med Henriette Hanck. 1830–46. Ved Svend Larsen. Copenhagen: E. Munksgaard, 1946 (Anderseniana IX–XIII, 1941–46).

H. C. Andersens Brevveksling med Jonas Collin den Ældre og andre medlemmer af det Collinske Hus. Udgivet af H. Topsoe-Jensen og under Medvirken af Kaj Bom og Knud Boegh. 3 vols. Copenhagen: E. Munksgaard, 1945–48.

H. C. Andersen og Henriette Wulff. En Brevveksling ved H. Topsoe-Jensen. 3 vols. Odense: Flendsted, 1959–60.

H. C. Andersens Brevveksling med Lucie og B.S.Ingemann. Udg. med indledning og kommentar af Kirsten Dreyer (Correspondence). 3 vols. Copenhagen: Museum Tusculanum forlag, Copenhagen University, 1997–98. http://www. kb.dk/elib/mss/hcabio/index.htm (Reconstituted biography of Andersen from his letters)

Journals

H. C. Andersens Dagboeger, 12 vols. Copenhagen: G.E.C. Gad, 1971–76.

Recent English Translation

Hans Christian Andersen: The Complete Stories. Trans. Jean Hersholt, preface Brian Alderson. London: The British Library, 2005.

Secondary Literature

Böök, Fredrik. *H. C. Andersen. En Levnadsteckning.* Copenhagen: Ascheboug, 1939.

Brandes, Georg. "Andersens Eventyr" (reprinted in Elias Bredsdorff, *H. C. Andersen og Georg Brandes.* Copenhagen: Ascheboug, 1994).

Bredsdorff, Elias. *Hans Christian Andersen. The Story of His Life and Work.* London: Phaidon/ New York: Scribner, 1975.

Groenbech, Bo. *H. C. Andersens Eventyrverden.* Copenhagen: P. Branner, 1945.

Hakon Rossel, Sven, ed. *Hans Christian Andersen: Danish Writer and Citizen of the World.* Amsterdam: Rodopi, 1996. http://www.andersen.sdu.dk/forskning/ index.html.

Joergensen, Aage. *H. C. Andersen-litteraturen 1875–1968,* Aarhus 1970, *and Andersen-litteraturen 1969–1994,* Odense 1995.

Mortensen, Klaus P. *Svanen og Skyggen—historien om unge Andersen.* Copenhagen: Gad, 1989.

Mylius, Johan de. *Myte og roman. H.C. Andersens romancer mellem romantic og realisme. En traditionshistorisk undersoegelse.* Odense: Gyldendal, 1981.

———. *H. C. Andersens liv. Dag for dag.* Odense: Aschehoug, 1998.

———, Aage Joergensen, and Viggo Hjoernager Pedersden. *Hans Christian Andersen: A Poet in Time.* Odense: Odense University Press, 1999.

Rubow, Paul V. *H. C. Andersens Eventyr. Forhistorien—Idé og Form—Sprog og Stil*. Copenhagen: Levin and Munksgaards, 1927.

Soerensen, Peer E. *H. C. Andersen og Herskabet. Studier I borgerlig krisebevidsthed*. Copenhagen: Forlaget GMT, 1973.

Topsoe-Jensen, Helge. *Mit eget Eventyr uden Digtning. En Studie over H. C. Andersen som Selvbiograf*. Copenhagen: Gyldendal, 1940.

Wullschlager, Jackie. *Hans Christian Andersen: The Life of a Storyteller*. London: A. A. Knopf, 2001.

List of Contributors

Elisa Biancardi (Università di Pavia, Italy) is the author of several articles on French précieux women writers: "De Madeleine de Scudéry à Mme d'Aulnoy: esthétique galante et merveilleux" (2002); "À propos de Mme d'Aulnoy: esthétique galante et genèse des contes de fées" (2002). She was also the editor of Champion's volume on Mme de Villeneuve and Mme Leprince de Beaumont in the "Bibliothèque des Génies et des fées": Madame de Villeneuve, *La Jeune Américaine et les contes marins; Les Belles Solitaires.* Madame Leprince de Beaumont, *Magasin des enfants* (2008). Recently she wrote an article on Leprince de Beaumont contrasting her life and her writings in an ideological point of view: « Contrapposizioni e compresenze logiche: "le sens le plus vrai" di Mme Leprince de Beaumont » (2010).

Ruth Bottigheimer (The State University of New York at Stony Brook), who published *Fairy Tales: A New History* with SUNY Press in 2009, earlier edited *Fairy Tales and Society: Illusion, Allusion, and Paradigm* (1986), *Gender and Story in South India* (2006), and *Fairy Tales, Printed Texts and Oral Tellings* (2007). She has examined the tales of the Brothers Grimm in *Grimms' Bad Girls and Bold Boys: The Moral and Social Vision of the Tales* (1987) and those of Giovan Francesco Straparola in *Fairy Godfather: Straparola, Venice, and the Fairy Tale Tradition* (2002), as well as the 800-year history of Bible stories rewritten for children's use in *The Bible for Children: From the Age of Gutenberg to the Present* (1996).

Nancy Canepa (Dartmouth College) edited the volume of essays *Out of the Woods: The Origins of the Literary Fairy Tale in Italy and France* (1997), and her critical work *From Court to Forest: Giambattista Basile's Lo cunto de li cunti and the Birth of the Literary Fairy Tale* (1999) received a number of awards, including a Modern Languages Association prize.

Her translations include Carlo Collodi's *The Adventures of Pinocchio* (2002), *Pinocchio* [film directed by Roberto Benigni] (2003), and *Giambattista Basile's The Tale of Tales, or Entertainment for Little Ones* (2007).

Jean-Pierre Collinet (deceased) (Université de Bourgogne, Dijon, France) published a modern edition of Charles Perrault's tales: Perrault. *Contes, suivis du Miroir ou La métamorphose d'Orante, De la Peinture, poème et du Labyrinthe de Versailles* (1981). A specialist of Jean de La Fontaine, he had published numerous pieces on that author, but mostly he was the author of Volume 1 of the Pléiade edition of La Fontaine's *Œuvres complètes*: "Fables, Contes et Nouvelles" (1991).

Manuel Couvreur (Université Libre de Bruxelles, Belgium) has published several pieces on the rapports between music, art, and literature in seventeenth- and eighteenth-century France. Since 2001, he has been working on Antoine Galland's unpublished travel reports, and he is currently working on the first French critical edition of Galland's *Arabian Nights: Les Mille et une nuit* (forthcoming 2011).

Donald Hettinga (Calvin College) is Professor of English and he teaches children's literature and writing. He is co-editor of *Sitting at the Feet of the Past: Retelling the North American Folktale for Children* and of the *Dictionary of Literary Biography: British Children's Writers, 1914–1960* (1992). He has also written *Presenting Madeleine L'Engle* (1993) and *The Brothers Grimm: Two Lives, One Legacy* (2001).

Shawn Jarvis (St. Cloud State University) contributed to *The Greenwood Encyclopedia of Folktales and Fairy Tales* (edited by Donald Haase, 2007), named by the *Library Journal* for inclusion on its list of Best Reference for 2007, and *The Oxford Companion to Fairy Tales: The Western fairy tale tradition from medieval to modern* (edited by Jack Zipes, 2001). She has also published two bibliophile editions in German of works by Gisela von Arnim (*Märchenbriefe and Achim*, 1990); and the first complete version, including unknown illustrations by Gisela and Herman Grimm, of the fairy-tale novel *Das Leben der Hochgräfin Gritta von Rattenzuhausbeiuns* (1986), both including critical commentary. She has also published translations of fairy tales by Gisela von Arnim and Caroline Stahl, as well as a first anthology in English of German women's fairy tales, *The Queen's Mirror: Fairy Tales by German Women Writers 1780–1900. An Anthology in English* (with Jeannine Blackwell, 2001).

Nadine Jasmin (Université Marc Bloch–Strasbourg II, France) is the author of a recent monograph on Madame d'Aulnoy: *Naissance du conte féminin. Mots et merveilles: les contes de fées de Madame d'Aulnoy* (2002). Jasmin is also the general editor of the "Bibliothèque des Génies et des fées," the first complete critical edition of fairy tales published in France in the period 1690–1789, an on-going 20 volume-collection published by the Paris editor Honoré Champion. In that collection, she edited the volume on Madame d'Aulnoy's fairy-tales: Madame d'Aulnoy. *Les Contes des Fées* suivis des *Contes nouveaux ou Les Fées à la Mode* (2004).

Geneviève Patard (Université d'Orléans, France) is the editor of Madame de Murat, *Contes* (2006) and she is the author of Madame de Murat's biographical entry on the SIEFAR (Société Internationale pour l'Etude des Femmes de l'Ancien Régime) Website: http://www.siefar.org/DicoA-Z.html (2008).

Sophie Raynard (The State University of New York at Stony Brook) published a monograph on the French *conteuses*: *La Seconde préciosité. Floraison des conteuses de 1690 à 1756*. (2002), as well as several articles on the poetics of seventeenth-century *conteuses* and on the interesting connections between the *conteuses*, preciosity, and libertinism. She also served as the guest editor for a special issue on fairy tales with the *Romanic Review: Approaches to the Literary Fairy Tales* (99:3–4). She is currently working on her second monograph on the poetics of early French fairy tales as expressed in their paratexts.

Yvette Saupé (non affiliated) published a monograph on Charles Perrault: *Les Contes de Perrault et la mythologie. Rapprochements et influences* (1997), and she contributed a modern edition of the Perrault brothers and Beaurain's *Les murs de Troye ou l'origine du burlesque, livre I* (2001).

Lewis Seifert (Brown University) is the author of *Fairy Tales, Sexuality, and Gender in France, 1690–1715: Nostalgic Utopias* (1996) and of *Manning the Margins: Masculinity and Writing in Seventeenth-Century France* (University of Michigan Press, 2009) as well as numerous articles on the *conteurs* and *conteuses* of seventeenth- and eighteenth-century France in a gender perspective.

Peer Soerensen (Aarhus Universitet, Denmark) published *H. C. Andersen og Herskabet. Studier I borgerlig krisebevidsthed* (1973).

Index